100 Huntley Street

The exciting success story
from the host
of Canada's popular television program,

100 Huntley Street

By David Mainse
With David Manuel

Logos International, Inc. Plainfield, NJ 07060
G.R.Welch Co., Ltd., Toronto, Ont.

The events in this book are true; only the
names of a few individuals have been changed,
in order to protect their privacy, or to avoid any
possible embarrassment.

I believe that Canada stands in a very unique position. If Canada should have a spiritual awakening and a revival, the whole world would look to her. Canada could become the world leader in a spiritual dimension.

—Billy Graham, on "100 Huntley Street"

Contents

FOREWORD

The most dynamic and far-reaching Christian work in Canada today, in my estimation, is emanating from a most unlikely source—an unassuming brick building in the heart of downtown Toronto, the address of which has become a household phrase: 100 Huntley Street. From that studio, a daily, phone-in Christian television show of the same name goes out to well over two-thirds of the population of Canada, and a growing number of UHF stations in the United States.

Also being produced in this studio are the live-action children's show, "Circle Square," which is carried weekly by one hundred fifty stations in Canada, the United States, Bermuda, Great Britain, Hong Kong and the Philippines; the teen show, "Inside Track," with as broad a coverage; the French language show, "Au 100 Tuple"; the new show just developed for the deaf, "Signs of the Times"; and the Christian talk show which was the forerunner of them all, "Crossroads." Those television stations which are carrying all of them are airing as many as twelve and a half hours of Christian programing a week!

Also there are regular Christian telecasts in Italian, "Vivere El Cento Per Cento," and seven others with titles around the 100 per cent living theme in German, Ukranian, Russian, Spanish, Portuguese, Chinese and Greek.

Even more exciting is the consistently high quality of the productions. It used to be that we Canadians had a national inferiority complex when it came to products stamped "Made in the USA." We assumed that anything could be made better, faster, and cheaper in the States.

Canadian Christians held to a similar assumption when they compared the things they created with the secular world's product. But the video programing coming out of 100 Huntley Street convincingly puts these assumptions to rest. In Edmonton, for instance, where there are three Canadian channels and three more brought in by cable from the States, 48 percent of all the sets turned on last month on a typical morning were tuned in to "100 Huntley Street"—and in St. Johns, Newfoundland, that figure was 89 percent, substantially more than all the other stations combined.

The fans of "100 Huntley Street" are a loyal bunch. In the two years it has been on the air, more than forty thousand visitors have been present in studio audiences, and over two hundred thousand phone calls have been received. Their official publication, *Direction*, goes out monthly to more than a hundred thousand subscribers in Canada and the United States, and there are, at last count, some six hundred phone counselors who are volunteering their time in seventeen counseling centers across the country. In addition to these, many other volunteers pay personal follow-up visits to those who have called in to accept Christ as their Saviour, or for healing and other helps rendered. Supporters of "100 Huntley Street" often drive long distances to attend annual regional rallies, an expression of the value they attach to the Christian work of the organization, which they demonstrably regard as the most democratic form of television there is. Supported entirely by voluntary contributions, it does not add a penny to the cost of a tube of toothpaste—or to one's annual income tax.

If there is a single theme that emerges from the work of 100 Huntley, it is that the body of Christ, traditionally fragmented into countless denominations and factions, can truly be one in the Spirit, joining together in fellowship and intercession, in praise and worship, and in testimony and evangelism. Having written my doctoral thesis at Oxford on the Ecumenical Movement, I would have to adjudge that nowhere else in Canada is there a stronger witness of genuine spiritual unity than in the ministry of "100 Huntley Street." This movement under God has taken a clear lead in calling Christians from coast to coast to unite in daily prayer for this country and for those in local and national authority, at this, the most critical moment in our history. For we will either come together in faith and love, or fall apart as a nation.

As I have indicated, it is impossible to assess the impact of the work being done by this small but dedicated group of people who are, for the most part, working for less than they could be earning in secular television. But ultimately all of this amazing fruit can be traced back to the obedience of one man who repeatedly had the courage to say "Yes, Lord," when God seemed to be asking the impossible. That individual is David Mainse, a small-town pastor to whom God gave the vision for national Christian television—and the grace.

I remember well the first time I appeared on David's program, "Crossroads." As founding chancellor of Richmond College, it gave me a chance to talk about the challenge of establishing a truly Christian liberal arts college in Canada. But we also talked about our shared conviction that in the last third of the twentieth century, the most effective vehicle with which to reach people is television. That has certainly proven true, and aside from our close personal friendship, there is no event of public witness I enjoy more than co-hosting with David on "100 Huntley Street."

In one sense, David is an extraordinary man of God. In another and deeper sense, he is really quite ordinary. He comes from a background no different than that of millions of other Canadians and Americans, with roots in a rural community which had Christ at its center and which called on its young men and women to do all things as unto the Lord. This is his story and the story of a unique and remarkable television ministry. But it is also the story of the heartland of Canada and the United States—of the deep values that have made these two countries great, and to which in spirit we must return, if we would recover our past glory. Yes, and we *can* return, if we will heed the example of the life unfolded in these pages.

John Wesley White
Summer, 1979

100 Huntley Street

CHAPTER 1

Ramsayville

As the cab turned down the street and made its way through the evening traffic, I glanced at my watch: 7:15. It would be close, but we were still on time. The light ahead of us turned red. Forcing myself to take a deep breath and relax, I looked out the window at Vancouver by night. Everywhere I could see, modern buildings reached up out of sight, each with attractive, well-lit shops at the base, and evening strollers passing by, bundled against the January chill. None of these buildings existed a generation ago, I mused, and I tried to imagine what downtown Vancouver must have looked like in 1936 when I was born. Were there a few old, two- or three-story brick buildings, as in Ottawa? It was incredible how fast we had grown, what a long ways Canada had come in such a short time.

The light turned green, and I looked again at my watch. Our rally was due to begin in ten, no, seven minutes. But now, up ahead, I could make out our destination, the gleaming marquee of the beautifully restored Orpheum Theatre—but what were all those people doing beneath it? Were those placards they were carrying? An icy knot formed in my stomach; these were pickets, marching and shouting, and as we drew closer, I could make out what their signs said, things like, "IF YOU LIKED HITLER, YOU'LL LOVE ANITA," and "BEING GAY IS A CULTURE, NOT A DISEASE" and "ANITA, WE'RE IN HEAVEN ALREADY!"

So the demonstration which we had anticipated in Toronto the week before and which had not materialized was now suddenly a very grim reality here. It explained the calls our Vancouver office had been receiving all day long, asking if Anita Bryant was going to be a surprise guest at our rally, as had been rumored. We had assured the callers and the media that she wasn't, and that we had no idea how those rumors had gotten started, but the homosexual community had obviously chosen not to believe us.

The Orpheum Theatre occupies one end of a city block, so I asked our driver to go around to the back entrance. All along the side of the theatre, men and women were marching, and as we passed by we could hear through the closed windows what they were chanting: "Gay rights now! Gay rights now!"

"Well, Lord," I murmured, "we're in your hands now," and I forced myself to give the whole situation over to Him.

The back entrance to the theatre was as crowded as the front. No sooner had I opened the door of the cab, than someone shouted, "There he is!" Getting out, I walked towards the bristling phalanx. All I could think of to say was, "I love you, and God loves you," and I said it loud enough for them to hear. Whatever they were expecting, that wasn't it; they parted ranks and made a path for me without comment. Before I knew it, I was inside and being shown to the dressing rooms behind the stage. Yes, I thought sadly, we had indeed come a long ways in a very short time.

Asking to be alone for a few minutes before joining the others on stage, I shut the door to the dressing room and sat down and closed my eyes. For some reason I thought of my uncle's farm in eastern Ontario, where I had spent my earliest years. I could see the barnyard and the corn field, and my uncle's horse, Mischief, pulling the one-furrow plow. I smiled, surprised at myself that I would pick such a time to reminisce. I hadn't thought of that place in years.

Shaking my head and taking a deep breath, I concentrated on clearing my mind and hearing whatever the Lord might want to give me in the way of a word for that evening. Through the door, I could hear the muffled strains of the old favorite, "He is Lord." It was time to go out and join the others.

That little farmhouse in Eastern Townships had a four-room addition on it, and for my mother and older sisters and me, for the duration of World War II, that addition was home. My father was a missionary in Egypt. He had been home on furlough for the first two years of my life, but in 1938, he felt called to return to Egypt, where he had spent the first seven years of his ordained ministry. Only this time he wasn't taking my mother with him. He perceived that the already precarious international situation might grow even more dangerous, and decided he had better go over alone, and send for the rest of us, when and if the situation showed any signs of stabilizing.

My father's discernment was unfortunately correct. Less than a month after he left, the Munich Pact was signed, and Czechoslovakia was delivered into Hitler's hands. Six months later, Albania fell to Mussolini, and for Poland, the handwriting was on the wall. A little less than a year after my father returned to his mission station in Asyut, Egypt, the German blitzkrieg was unleashed, and the dark clouds of war encircled the globe. My father would not be able to return home until the end of 1944, six years after his departure. He could do nothing but consign his family into the Lord's hands while he was about his Father's business, and trust that God would take care of us.

My earliest memory is of a tricycle I was given for Christmas in 1939, four months after I had turned three. It was an old, beat-up one, but it was the first thing like it I had ever had. I was overjoyed and proceeded to wear a path in the linoleum that covered the floor of our two downstairs rooms. Out to the kitchen and around the table, then back into the living room and around the couch, and back to the kitchen again. About the only time my mother could get me off of it was for meals, and even then I would be back riding again before the meal was over. For she and my two older sisters, Willa and Elaine, had considerable difficulty getting me to finish my bread crusts, and would use the tricycle as a bribe. I would take the detested crust in hand, pretending to be eating it, and would wheel into the living room, returning a short while later empty-handed and with a big grin, accepting everyone's enthusiastic approval.

I got away with it for quite a while, until the day my mother moved the couch to scrub the floor, and to her horror discovered a sizable pile of nibbled crusts, nibbled not by me but by the field mice which had found their way into our home, attempting to escape the winter cold. That escapade earned me another first: my introduction to the switch. In later years, I would not infrequently renew the acquaintanceship, for where discipline was concerned I was a handful—often literally.

My two older sisters had to both hold me down, while my mother administered the daily spoonful of cod liver oil which she was convinced was the only thing that stood between me and deadly pneumonia during the wintertime. But generally, it took something as gravely serious as a lie to merit the switch, and when I was older, I was given the psychological punishment of having to go cut the switch she would use. Needless to say, if it wasn't large enough, I was sent back out for another.

There was only one offense worse than lying, and that was stealing. Seared forever into my memory—as my mother intended it should be—was what happened one July afternoon in 1943. Between our place and the general store was the Burns's farm which had a sand-fill area ideal for playing with my toy trucks. I went over there after school one afternoon, and did a good deal of miniature earth-moving and road-grading, in the course of which I found a spoon and pocketed it, without paying much attention to it.

My mother paid a great deal of attention to it, however, when I got home and curiously brought it out of my pocket. It wasn't long before I was sent to find a switch as big around as my thumb and, worse, I had to go back and tell Mrs. Burns I had stolen her spoon, give it back to her, and ask her forgiveness. Needless to say, that sort of lesson lasted a long, long time.

The vast majority of my memories are sunny, however. We were very poor in those days, but I didn't know it. There was always enough to eat, and always fresh vegetables from our garden. A substantial garden was a must, I learned later; we had to make do on the five dollars a week the missionary board paid us. We had some hens of our own in a little coop alongside the addition and there were always fresh eggs, and Uncle Harvey had a couple of old cows, which kept us in milk. My favorite of all the chores was to turn the handle of the milk separator, which separated the cream so that it could be taken to the creamery to be made into cheese. My reward was to remove the lid and scoop up a cup of the warm froth. Young people are fond of Fribbles and Frostees and all manner of exotic milkshakes, but I can't imagine them tasting any better than a cup of freshly turned froth.

Summers were the best times. We started going barefoot almost as soon as the frost left the ground, and didn't put shoes on again until the leaves began to fall (except for church, of course). There was a creek running by the back of Uncle Harvey's property, and there was a wide place for wading and water fights. Swimming was a special treat for really hot afternoons. We played other games mostly in the evening, after supper, because we were busy doing farm work during the day. Some of the games which we played with John and Marian White, who lived on the next farm, included tag, kick-the-can, and antie-aye-over, where one side would throw the ball over the house, calling out, "antie-aye-over" just before winging it. It was tricky because you never knew quite where the ball would be coming from. The other player on your side would keep score and then it would be his turn. The last game of the evening was invariably hide-and-seek, which was my favorite because we played in the dusk, just before it was time to go to bed, and it was dark enough to really hide.

I began doing chores when I was four years old; I would go out in the morning with the egg basket, and I loved to reach under the soft, fuzzy warmth of each hen, to see if there was an egg. But there was one mean, old, one-eyed hen who would try to peck my hand. She pecked me a couple of times before I learned to snap my fingers with one hand while reaching under her with the other.

I'll never forget the day Uncle Harvey first let me try to dig a furrow behind old Mischief. I was all of six, and so proud I must have grown an inch in twenty minutes. Uncle Harvey solemnly handed me the lines and told me to keep my eye on a certain fence post at the far end of the field, in order to plow straight. I tried to hide my impatience, for I had walked alongside him many an afternoon as he plowed, picking up any suitable fishing worms he turned up. So I nodded as he explained, hurrying him up, and then he stepped behind me and put his hands on the handles, "All right, David, let's go."

I shook the lines and made the twitching sound I had heard him so often make, and Mischief started up, giving a snort; for a moment I could have sworn she was laughing at me. I squinted to keep the post in sight over Mischief's hind quarters, and almost before I knew it, we had reached the end of the row, and it was time to turn and start back. When I did, I stopped, stunned. All the furrows were ribbon-straight except for the one I had done, which weaved and staggered all over the place. Uncle Harvey never chuckled or said a word, and I loved him for that.

Saturday night was bath night, so that we would be clean for church the next morning. One of my assignments was to keep the wood box by the kitchen stove filled, and as soon as I was eight, I was allowed to use the axe to split the logs as well. I was tremendously proud of this and would spend a fair amount of Saturday afternoon chopping and splitting and making kindling, laying in a good supply, for the water reservoir at the end of the stove would need to be as hot as it could be.

Then, after supper and Bible reading, we would bring out the old galvanized tub. We placed it as close to the stove as possible for warmth, especially on winter nights, when the temperature outside was well below zero, and the relentless wind made it colder still. The tub was filled with water as hot as a body could stand, and we had more standing by in the big kettle on the stove, for rewarming the tub. I got to go first, so I could clear out and leave the kitchen to the women. I remember we used homemade soap, and mother always used to check to see if I had gotten clean enough behind the ears.

The biggest treat of the summer was to go "down to the corners" with mother and Aunt Mina and have an ice cream cone, while they shopped in the general store. The store had one flavor, vanilla, and nothing on earth tasted so good as the first lick, sitting at the cool, dark marble counter. On special occasions, like Dominion Day, or when company came, we made our own at home, and that ice cream, cold and smooth, was wonderful too. But somehow the luxury of being able to just sit there on that stool and not having to turn the crank or anything, and having a crunchy cone at the end, with ice cream packed down in it, right to the bottom, made this the best of all possible treats. I didn't sit still for long, but was soon off my stool, treasured cone in hand, and out the swinging screen door to look around town.

The village was called Ramsayville, after the family who owned the biggest farm in the area and also the general store. It was really just a crossroads, with the store, two churches, and the blacksmith's shop which had also become a garage with a gas pump. Harry Smith ran it, and he both fixed cars and shoed horses. The rest of the time that mother and Aunt Mina were in the store, I would spend watching Harry. Sometimes, walking home, we would encounter old Dave, who was always chewing tobacco and spitting it everywhere, and letting a little dribble down his unshaven chin, especially if any of the good ladies of the village were present. He so scandalized my mother that she insisted I be called *David* and would not permit anyone to use the shorter version.

The worst part of summer, of course, was the end of it, and the beginning of school. That meant Willa and Elaine would go off to the one-room schoolhouse which was just down the road from us, on the other side of our corn field, and would be gone all day long. It was worse the summer I turned four, for I was old enough to enjoy their company (though I am not sure the feeling was reciprocated, as they were six and eight years older than me). That year, on the first day of school, I stood in the far corner of the field and watched them walk by, not saying anything to them, just watching with tears streaming down my cheeks.

But that winter, when it was too cold to play outside after supper, they taught me how to read and write and how to add and subtract, so I felt even unhappier at the end of the summer when I turned five, and they again went off. This time I didn't go to the far corner of the field, but waited by the house, trying to pretend I was not interested in their leaving, but craning to see them disappearing down the road.

Long after they were out of sight, I stared in the direction of the school, sad and lonely, but not crying this year, for bawling was baby stuff. All of a sudden I thought I saw Elaine climbing through the fence. It *was* Elaine, and she was running across the field shouting something. It wasn't bad news; she was waving and grinning. "David! David! Get your good shirt on; you're going to school!"

"I'm *what?*" But she ran right past me and into the house to tell mother. "Willa and I talked to Miss Bice," she panted, out of breath. "We told her we'd taught David the beginnings of reading and writing and arithmetic, and said he'd be no trouble, and she said we could bring him."

My mother looked down at me, a frown furrowing her brow. "Well, all right," she said at length, "but you'd better not be any trouble, David Mainse!" And off to school I went.

But telling me to stay out of trouble was like telling a puppy not to bark. Trouble just came naturally to me, and with no father at home to speak truth to me by hand, I got into a good deal more than my share at school. One of the problems was that I had already learned more than the other first graders I was with, and so all that year and for the next two, I was much more interested in eavesdropping on what the seventh and eighth graders were learning in history and social studies, since ours was a one-room schoolhouse with fifty-two pupils in it.

One incident the following year stands out in my memory. It happened on the first really warm day of April, when the windows were open, and the afternoon air was soft and mellow with the smells of spring. You could hear the crickets, and in the distance I could see Uncle Harvey and Mischief, going back and forth. Miss Bice had already called my attention back more than once, and I could see her eyebrows arch over her steel-rimmed glasses, as she periodically glanced in my direction. I tried to get interested in what Dick and Jane were doing with their dog Spot, but it just wasn't very exciting.

I do not know what first drew my attention to it, but the right pigtail of the girl who sat in front of me came amazingly close to my inkwell every time she leaned back in her seat, which she did fairly often as she, too, was having trouble concentrating. Funny, she had been sitting in front of me all year, and I had never noticed that before. I wondered what would happen if I were to take off the top of my inkwell and just sort of lift her pigtail over the front of my desk and into the waiting receptacle.

Here she came, leaning back again. I looked up to make sure Miss Bice was well occupied with the older kids up in front of the room, then silently took the top off the inkwell and gently lifted the pigtail clear of the edge of the desk. Charlie Murray sat at the desk next to mine, and his eyes widened as he saw what I intended to do. I held the pigtail lightly in my hand, waiting for her to lean back just a little more. Then she did, and I guided the pigtail deep into the inkwell.

At that Charlie let out a gasp of stifled glee, too late clapping a hand over his mouth. Miss Bice was on me in an instant, her fury cold and even, which was far more frightening. She took me into the washroom, got down the strap, and laid it to me. The humiliation was far more painful than the strap itself, but even so, Miss Bice was one of the best teachers I ever had, and to this day I have the greatest respect for her.

Sunday was my favorite day of the week, even though we weren't allowed to do anything like play ball or go swimming. The Lord had declared it was to be a day of rest, and our church took Him literally, not sanctioning any work, let alone play, that was not absolutely necessary. We belonged to a denomination called "The Holiness Movement," with about fifty congregations in eastern Ontario and Quebec which had sprung out of the Methodist tradition during the previous century. We were like some of the Mennonite groups in some ways, though we were not quite as severe as they were about outward adornment. But we did take our worship very seriously and had prayer at the family altar after each meal and again kneeling by our beds at night. And there was Bible reading once a day, usually after supper.

In the summertime, we would walk to church or take the buggy, but in the winter, the roads would be so full of snow as to be impassable, so Uncle Harvey would hitch up Mischief to the cutter and bundle us all under a huge buffalo robe, with heated up clothes irons on the floorboards to keep our feet warm on the way. I loved the bells and the chinking sound of the harness and the crunch of the runners as they bit through the snow. And I would peep out of the buffalo robe to watch the ice-sheathed branches as they passed by.

As was the case in school, I had some difficulty keeping my attention where it belonged, and occasionally our pastor, the Reverend Stewart Woodland, would have to rebuke me from the pulpit. He understood my mother's situation, and did what he could to be a male influence in my life, taking me with him from time to time when he had business in Ottawa six miles away. The road went by the provincial prison, and every time we passed it, he would intone somberly: "That's where you're going to wind up, David, if you don't behave." It made a deep impression, as did his warning, "If you keep worrying your mother, I'll take the gad to you." I never did learn exactly what the "gad" was, but I knew it was something I never wanted to have taken to me.

The church was cold those wintry mornings but it had an old pot-bellied stove, and the families in the nearest pews got the most heat. Rev. Woodland had no trouble encouraging promptness in the wintertime. One of the things that fascinated me about our church was watching Barber Quinn. Very much in the Wesleyan tradition of expressing his approval during a sermon, Barber Quinn didn't content himself with just an occasional spontaneous "amen." If the preacher hit a really strong note, Barber Quinn whooped and vaulted over the pew in front of him, then walked around and sat back down in his seat. And you never knew quite when it was going to happen. So whenever the preacher really got into it, I kept my eyes on Barber Quinn to see if the sermon was going to be a whooper.

There was another elderly gentleman who sat in the back, whom I would occasionally crane around to watch. His name was Sid Ridgeway. I sensed that most of our congregation felt Sid's spiritual status was not quite what it ought to be. He had a set of false teeth, and when everyone else would say amen, Sid would push his false teeth out so you could see his gums, and then suddenly suck them back in again. Once I started watching, I couldn't take my eyes off him, until I would hear mother's sharp whisper, "David!"

9

When church was over, we went home to Sunday dinner, the big meal of the week. There would be a roast, mashed potatoes and gravy, and fresh-baked bread steaming from the oven, and fresh, sweet butter and home-canned vegetables from the garden (there seemed to be an endless supply of Ball jars on shelves in the root cellar), and pickle preserves to go with the meat, and for dessert, a homemade apple or mince pie.

After dinner, one of my sisters would read our denomination's Sunday school newsletter, *Young People's Guide*, to the other two of us, and we would listen with rapt attention that sometimes got unrapt as drowsiness overtook us. Later in the afternoon, I would usually take a walk down by the creek. In the late spring and summertime I chafed under not being able to play ball or swim, but I came to love these walks, and got so that I could identify all the trees and flowers by name—trillium and jack-in-the-pulpits were the two blooms in greatest abundance. Sometimes I would skip a stone along the surface of the creek or just watch the running water and let my mind wander. At times like that, as I grew older, I wondered what my father was like. There was the picture of him on mom's dresser, of course, but I couldn't tell much from it. He had a strong face with a high forehead and square jaw, and he looked like he might be physically very powerful. My mother assured me that although he did not talk a lot, he was the kindest, best man she knew.

At any rate, I was not going to be long in finding out. It was November, 1944, and we knew from his letters that he would soon be arriving home. I was excited, but I was also shy—and vaguely uneasy in a way I didn't fully understand. I was eight years old now, and had been the man of the house ever since I could remember. What was it going to be like having dad home?

I was going to find out even sooner that I thought. There was a commotion in the house, and Elaine called from the door, "Dad's on Aunt Mina's phone! He's in Ottawa, and will be home in an hour!"

CHAPTER 2

Training Us Up

"He's coming!" Elaine shouted and I grimaced. I was disgusted with both her and Willa, who had been carrying on ever since the phone call, getting more and more excited. And mother had been no help; if anything, she seemed to be encouraging them! And now—"He's *here*!" Elaine shrieked.

I took one look at the tall, deeply tanned figure striding up the drive and did a very uncharacteristic thing. I ran and hid behind some bushes—I was doubly embarrassed, because now, sooner or later, I would have to emerge. Sooner as it turned out: "David?" It was my mother calling and I knew I had no choice. Smiling somewhat shamefacedly, I revealed myself and came hesitantly forward. My father seemed oblivious to my unsocial behavior. He scooped me up in his arms and gave me a big hug and just held me for a while. This impressed me, because I was large for my eight years and must have weighed a good eighty pounds. He was as strong as I had imagined.

With everyone talking at once, we went inside and sat in the living room, and Willa and Elaine proceeded to try to tell him everything that had happened in the last six years. "It's good to be home," was the sum total of his response, but he said it with a big grin, and he took my mother and sat her on his knee. It was an unusual display of public affection, and the only one I would ever see him make, for my father was a proper Victorian in many ways.

We had the month of December together. My father was anxious to get to know his family again, and so did not volunteer for a pastorate or home mission work. He did volunteer to help our next-door neighbor, Mr. White, who, for the last few years before dad came home, had provided us with free milk every day, because Uncle Harvey's old cows had given out and been slaughtered. Dad said he could not do enough to repay Mr. White, who later told me that dad worked harder than any man he had ever known. That was the beginning of the broadening of my ecumenical outlook, for Mr. White belonged to the United Church.

Mr. White was also chairman of the local school board, which had a problem on its hands. Our teacher in the one-room schoolhouse (Miss Bice's successor) had had to leave at the end of the semester, and they were hard-pressed to find a replacement. The board asked my father if he would be the interim teacher until the end of the school year in June. As both Elaine and I were still in that school and my mother offered to help with grades one through four, he felt he could accept without compromising his basic intent of getting to know his family again.

From the day of my father's return, my mother's discipline problems with me were over. Never one for spoiling the child, my father spared the rod neither at home nor at school. Whenever there was a disturbance, no matter who caused it, he usually included me in the strapping, and I suspected he was making up in six months for the six years he had been away. In any event, I soon saw the error of my ways and became the most law-abiding citizen in that school.

The thing I remember most about my father in school was not the discipline or his teaching ability (and he was a fine teacher), but his sciatica and the lengths he had to go to obtain a measure of relief from pain. He had been in southern Egypt for most of his recent tour, and had gotten used to a hot, dry climate. Now, suddenly immersed in the cold and wet of an Ontario winter, his joints ached unmercifully, and the only way he could get relief was to lie down and stretch out on a hard, flat surface. The trouble was, with fifty-two of us in that one room, there was no floor space large enough to accommodate him. So, as soon as he had all the children busily at work, he would get up on the old grand piano and stretch out on it, telling us why he was doing it, of course.

Dad continued to suffer cruelly until Easter Sunday afternoon. He had been asked to say the benediction at the afternoon service of the Young People's Easter Convention in Ottawa. When the time for the benediction came, he hurt so badly that he could barely get to his feet. As he described it later, the sides of his arms and legs and the heels of his feet felt as sore as if they were covered with boils. Nevertheless, he got up and began to pray. "All of a sudden, the blessing of high heaven flooded my soul, and the resurrection life of Christ completely healed me! In one second I was perfectly well, praise His dear Name!" (The one place where dad was not reticent was when it came to praising God.) I didn't know much about the blessing of high heaven at that point, but there was no question that he was no longer plagued with sciatica. In fact, I think the kids at school were a little disappointed that he no longer needed to get up on the grand piano.

Needless to say, there were some significant changes on the home front too. We started doing our Bible reading at breakfast, and ten o'clock at night was curfew. For me, that meant homework done, prayers said, and lights out. But it meant bedtime for the adults as well. It didn't matter who might be visiting or how lovely the summer evening might be; when ten o'clock came, my father would clear his throat, and everybody knew that was the signal for the evening to come to a close.

With the coming of June, my father was asked by the ministerial stationing committee of our denomination to take a circuit of his own in Madoc, a little rural village on the Trans-Canada Highway, about halfway between Toronto and Ottawa. He accepted, although to me it seemed about as far away from anything as it was possible to get. But my father never complained about any of his assignments and if he was disappointed now he gave no indication. He accepted it as God's will for him and determined to do his best as always.

It meant we would be leaving the only place I had known as home, and while I was happy we would have a home of our own, I was sad to be leaving. Just before we left, I took a last look around, going into the barn to say goodbye to Mischief. I brought her a carrot, as I usually did, and then turned away from her stall quickly before I started to cry.

I stopped and gazed high above at the rough-hewn crossbeams that stretched from one side of the barn to the other. I thought back to the first time I had crawled across one of those beams. I had been about seven, and half scared out of my wits when there was no longer piled-up hay in the loft underneath me, but stables and concrete floors. But later I had done it again and again, until I was hardly scared at all. Happily, our good-byes with Uncle Harvey and Aunt Mina were not prolonged, and before I knew it we were on our way.

Our home in Madoc was a modest one. With six rooms it was considerably more spacious and luxurious than we had been accustomed to. The village itself numbered scarcely fifteen hundred yet seemed huge after Ramsayville, though perhaps a twentieth of them could be counted on to be in the pews of our church on a given Sunday.

The size of his congregation did not dismay my father. He prepared his sermons as carefully as if he anticipated ten times that number. As long as he was illustrating his sermons with anecdotes, I liked to listen to the preaching. But the rest of the time, I was either restless and fooling around or falling asleep. My dad did not hesitate to reprimand me from the pulpit—"David, I'll deal with you later!"—or ask me questions to see if I was paying attention.

But I did love his stories, and perhaps the one which made the deepest impression on me was what happened to his older brother Charlie when Charlie was four. My grandfather had been a farmer, and one January he had taken the wooden pump out of the well to have some repairs made on it. He had headed for town with the pump, leaving the well covered with a large board. My Uncle Charlie apparently had an inquisitive bump, as my father put it; he wanted to see what was under that board. So he pushed it off, stuck his head in, and next thing you know he fell right in.

After a while, his mother missed her lad and started looking for him, growing increasingly worried. Finally she saw him, crawling out of the horse stable on his hands and knees. She ran to him and found that he was soaking wet, and so cold he couldn't speak. She ran with him into the house, then ran back out to the road and called for her brother-in-law, Edward, who lived on the next farm. When Edward saw the boy, he hitched up a horse and rode off to town to get the doctor. In the meantime, Charlie's mother built up the fire in the stove, changed his wet clothes, and wrapped him in blankets.

By the time Edward returned with Dr. Cregan, Charlie was getting so that he could speak, though his lips were still blue and his teeth chattering.

"Well, son," the doctor said, "what happened to you?"

"Fell in the well," he managed to reply.

"How did you get out?" the doctor asked.

"I tried to climb up, but it was too slippery and cold, and I fell back in again. I saw I was going to die, and so I asked the Lord to help me. He came down, put His arms underneath me, and lifted me out of there and set me on top of the well."

Dr. Cregan didn't say anything for a moment; then he looked at my grandfather. "I want to see that well," he said.

The two men went out to the well, and the doctor asked Charlie's father to go down in it and see how deep it was and how much water was in it. Charlie's father did, stretching his legs to reach both sides at once, and barely able to find stones jutting out on which to get a foothold. It was sixteen feet down to the water, and the water was six feet deep in the well.

When he reemerged, he had Charlie's little straw hat with him, which he had fished out of the water, and which he handed to Dr. Cregan without speaking. The doctor took it and just shook his head. "It's a miracle," he said slowly, "a miracle!"

That story never failed to move me, and I have since used it countless times myself to help young children understand the reality of God. But my father's favorite stories were those of his mission field in Egypt, where a whole congregation would be so moved that they would dance for joy and sing with equal enthusiasm. One day a blind beggarwoman from Ghaniam named Bakeeta happened to be in Bagoor and heard the singing. She asked a passerby what it was, and when she was told, she went into the mission herself and gave her life to Jesus. Shortly afterwards, she had a friend send a letter to the mission, asking for a preacher of God's Word to be sent to her village of Ghaniam, to hold meetings such as the one she had experienced in Bagoor.

But there was no one to send, and the superintendent of missions sent a reply saying so. Bakeeta sent another letter, and the superintendent sent another regretful reply. Once more, Bakeeta wrote, and this time she said she would give her life's savings from begging, fifty dollars, to support a preacher, for she was convinced that by the time it was gone, there would be enough people converted to support a permanent preacher in Ghaniam.

The superintendent could no longer deny such faith; a young Egyptian preacher was assigned to Ghaniam, and my father offered to help pioneer the work. My father preached for three Sundays, and prayed and talked with the brethren in between. After three weeks, so many were converted that he formed a society which pledged itself to support the pastor and blind Bakeeta, who never had to go back to begging.

I had no trouble concentrating on stories like that one, but unfortunately, the glory of the Lord was still a Sunday thing for me. I liked the things of God well enough in our prayer times at home and in our Bible reading, but they had no real grip on my life, especially when I was in the company of my peers. I had just turned nine that fall of 1945, and one afternoon I was walking home after school with some of my new classmates. As we approached Mr. Kincaid's grocery store, the other guys, knowing I was a P.K. (preacher's kid), dared me to take one of the apples that were in a box out front. I didn't want to, but they made it clear that the new boy in school was going to be mocked as a sissy all year if he didn't take one. So I did, snatching one, and dashing around the corner. I kept on running, heading for home and eating the evidence as I ran.

I threw away the core, just before I came in sight of the house, and tried to look nonchalant as I walked in the front door. "How did school go today?" mother asked, cocking her head ever so slightly as she looked at me.

"Oh, fine," I replied noncommittally, concentrating on a recipe that was on the kitchen counter.

"David," she said, "look at me. There's something wrong."

But looking at her was the last thing I wanted to do. How did she *always* seem to know?

"David, what's the trouble? What have you done?"

"I haven't done *anything,* mother," I answered, trying to work up some vestige of righteousness at being so unfairly accused.

"You're not going to tell me?"

"There's nothing to tell," I lied, growing progressively more miserable.

"Come into the bedroom, David; there's something wrong; and we need to get down on our knees and pray to see what it is."

Scarcely had my knees touched the floor than I began to sob. Soon it was all out in the open, and I wished I could have died, I was so ashamed. I remembered Mrs. Burns's spoon vividly though that was several years before, and when mother asked God to forgive me, I felt I was going to drop into hell any minute. To my mixed anguish and relief she told me that I was going to pay for that apple with my own money. She figured ten cents would cover it, which was about double the going rate in those days, and I was going to have to tell Mr. Kincaid what I had done and ask his forgiveness.

At that, I dissolved into wails of despair and begged to be allowed to just write it in a note and put it in an envelope, rather than have to tell him face to face. My mother relented on that point, and I went and wrote the note:

> Dear Mr. Kincaid:
>   I took an apple from the box and I'm sorry and here's the money to pay for it.
>   David Mainse

Out the door I went, alone. There was no need for my mother to come; she would know if I had done it or not when I got home. At Kincaid's Grocery, Mr. Kincaid, a big man in a white apron, was chatting with a customer at the check-out counter. I started to wait until he was free, but my resolve, shaky to begin with, grew steadily weaker. Finally, I just shoved the envelope, which had his name on it, under a large box of cornflakes on the counter, and hastily left.

No sooner had I gotten home than the phone rang. Mother answered it, spoke for a moment, then turned to me, "It's Mr. Kincaid. He wants you to come back to the store."

My heart plummeted down to shoe-top level. Was this nightmare never going to end? Eyes brimming, I turned without a word and trudged slowly back to the store. When I got there, I kept my gaze on the floor; I couldn't bring myself to look Mr. Kincaid in the eye.

"David, look at me." I forced myself to comply—and was surprised to see him smiling. "You have done a very brave thing—in fact, the finest thing I have ever known a boy to do. You were wrong to take the apple, but you then confessed it and did the right thing. I want you to know this: as long as you remain in Madoc, you can have a job delivering groceries for me, if you want one."

I could not believe my ears. "You mean—a job? Of my own?"

"Yep, I checked it with your mother."

"Wow—when can I start?"

"Right now, if you like. I have a delivery ready to go to Mrs. Rankin up on the hill."

And so began my first venture into free enterprise. It soon developed that I had a rather unusual entrepreneurial bent. For instance, I heard Mr. Kincaid mention that he wished he had some six-quart and three-quart baskets to put fruit in. No sooner said than done. I offered to buy from the persons I delivered to any old baskets they might have.

They were so taken with the prospect of this nine-year-old budding businessman that they made a special effort to find and save old baskets. I paid one penny apiece for them and Mr. Kincaid paid me two cents for the smaller ones and three for the larger ones—until I had brought in so many he no longer needed them.

Now that I had the hang of capitalism, my next venture was more ambitious: Christmas trees. It was getting on towards Christmas, and it seemed to me that most people were too busy to think about getting a tree until the last minute, when they would rush to the florist or the lumberyard and make their selections from the scraggly lot that were left. So I borrowed a toboggan and each day after school took my axe and went back into the bush. An hour or two later, I would return with three or four felled trees tied to the toboggan and then I would peddle them door to door. And since they were full and bushy, I never failed to get a good price for them. Before long, I had more cash than I had ever possessed in my life. I was so proud of myself, I couldn't wait to tell my father. But when I did, his response was hardly what I had anticipated. "Where did you get them?" he asked, a frown crossing his brow.

"In the field by the road. Why?"

"Didn't it occur to you that they might belong to someone?"

"What do you mean? You and I used to go out, cutting firewood every Saturday last winter, whatever we needed."

"But I had made arrangements with the man who owned the woods to do that."

Slowly the truth sank in, and I was crestfallen. My father was stern that afternoon but he wasn't angry. He said he would take me in the car (we had a secondhand Chevy now), I would show him where I cut the trees, and we would make reparations with the owner, whatever that meant.

When we found the farmer's house, he was at home—and very gracious. He smiled and said, "Oh, that's all right; I never would have done anything with them anyhow." And I even got to keep the money. But from that point forth, I had a healthy respect for other people's property.

One other thing happened that Christmas that made a lasting impression. During the Christmas holidays, I decided to work. I would go from house to house, offering to do odd jobs, like splitting and stacking firewood or shoveling snow. I never put a price on my labor, leaving people to pay me whatever they felt I had earned, and I usually wound up with about fifty cents for a day. It wasn't much, but it was fair, because I was only nine and not able to do the work of a grown man.

I got my biggest job on the last day of the year. A house had received a truckload of firewood, and the man of the house told me I could come back the next day and stack it all neatly in the woodshed, because it had been left in a huge pile by the side of his house. Elated, I told my mother of the windfall, and she said fine, but to be sure to be back in time for supper. So I got to work early the next afternoon, and I must have been at it about three hours when the man came out of the house. And he was so happy—so happy he didn't notice how cold it was, even with no coat on. He came over and put his arm around my shoulders and. giggled and said, "Oh, you poor boy, working so hard on New Year's Day. Here, take this and be gone with you; you can finish up tomorrow." And to my astonishment, he pressed a bill into my hand. And when I opened it, I was dumbfounded: it was a *ten*-dollar bill! I looked up to see if he realized what he had given me, but he just nodded and smiled and made his way somewhat irregularly back into the house.

I stood there for a moment, then dashed off home. "Mother, mother!" I shouted, as I banged into the kitchen. "Look!" and I held up the bill. Dad came in, and the two of them asked me to tell them about it. When I did, they looked knowingly at one another, and then dad said, "I think he must have been celebrating New Year's Day, David, drinking liquor, which makes a man take leave of his senses and do foolish things. He probably didn't know what he was doing, and I'm sure he can't afford to give you ten dollars. You're going to have to take it back, son."

And so, once again I trudged through the snow back to the house and knocked at the door. This time a lady answered, and when I explained what had happened, she thanked me profusely and took the ten dollars back. "Wait here a moment," she said, and ducked inside the house. She quickly returned with something in her hand. "This is for your work," she said and handed me two quarters, though I had done only three hours' work. She thanked me again, murmuring that she would certainly have something to say to her husband when he woke up.

My parents continued to train me up in the way they intended me to go, and while at times I was disappointed or I chafed under their authority, I recall that year in Madoc as a tremendously happy one. I say year, singular, because that was what it was. In June, the board of

Annesley College, which was the seminary of our denomination, asked my father if he would asume the position of principal, which had to be the most prestigious post in the whole denomination, except for the job of superintendent itself! I was so proud of my father, I could have burst. But if he was pleased, he showed no more sign of it than he had the year before when we had been sent to Madoc.

And so, in the summer of 1946, the Mainse family moved from a little farm town in southern Ontario to the nation's capital. Imagine: we were moving to the home of the Ottawa Rough Riders, one of the best teams in pro football! Could there be a more exciting place for a ten-year-old to live?

CHAPTER 3

Annesley

It has been my custom when a challenging idea presents itself not to be discouraged simply because it has never been done before or because the experts say it is impossible, but to pursue it and see if it cannot be brought into reality. Nowadays, I hope that such ideas are from the Lord, along with the ability to perceive and pursue them. But my tenacity seems to trace back to before I knew Him as my personal Saviour.

Take the Ottawa Rough Riders, for instance. Every boy my age in eastern Ontario would have given his eyeteeth to be their "go-fer." ("Say, Davey, go fer a cup of coffee, would ya?") But instead of just dreaming about it, I went over to the old stadium where the Rough Riders played, which was only a block away from Annesley, and hung around the door to the locker room. I would offer to go to the drugstore for tape or aspirins, or anything they needed, and, after a while, they invited me in. Gradually I became a fixture around the place. My hero at that time was Tony Golab, and I made up my mind that I too would play football when I got big enough.

On Sundays, when they had a home game, they used to run in together through the big gate at the end of the field, and they told me to run with them, in the middle of them. I did this, peeling off after they got to their benches, and going up into the stands. Occasionally, a guard would chase me, but I figured the football players were the most important people there and they owned the place, so how could anyone else say anything?

For the next two years, I was the Rough Riders' unofficial "go-fer," and I was on the hustle elsewhere as well. On Saturdays, I got a job as the Walker bread man's house runner. We would start at six in the morning, and he would let me drive the horse, which I loved, until the wagon reached the residential area. Then I would be off and running up the driveways, depositing the bread in the milk chutes and picking up the money and next week's orders. We would finish about noon, and the rest of Saturday, except on home game days, I would spend on my bike, delivering for the Flora Printers, our denomination's print shop which also published the *Young People's Guide*. They used to do letterheads and stationery, and catered to the members of Parliament, which meant I had a number of deliveries to make in the Parliament building. Most people might resent having to climb five flights, but not me. The Parliament building had beautiful brass bannisters, *unbroken* by any knobs or newel posts at the corners, so that as countless boys on school trips must have noted, it was theoretically possible to slide from the top all the way to the bottom without stopping.

Well, as I have indicated, I was one for putting theory into practice, and in those days security in the building was far less tight than it is now. I would climb on at the top (and I mean going up one flight to start on the sixth floor) and then let her rip, slowing only at the corners to see if anyone was coming, and to keep from flying off from centrifugal force.

But perhaps my greatest entrepreneurial coup occurred the last two weeks of each August. Annesley College owned an empty lot that was almost kitty-corner to the exhibition grounds of the Central Canada Exhibition. I would rent the property from Annesley for that two-week period and hire younger kids to run down the street with signs, shouting "Parking, Parking for the Ex!" In no time, the lot would be full of cars, and after expenses, I would clear two hundred to three hundred dollars, a small fortune in those days.

To balance such energetic but worldly enthusiasm, there was always the formality of life at home. Annesley College had an enrollment of about thirty students at any one time, and my father was instructor as well as principal. His main concern was to prepare these young men for ministerial positions, the mission field, or just for living mature Christian lives. To his way of thinking, that had as much to do with building character as it did with assimilating head knowledge. At the same time, mother concentrated on their table manners and getting them accustomed to dining in gracious surroundings, so that if they were invited into fine homes, they would not bring disgrace to themselves—or the denomination. Consequently, students were required to wear coats and ties to the evening meal, which was served on good china, with white tablecloths and silver and stemware completing the scene. The room lent itself to an aura of genteel dining, for the building the college occupied had once been one of the grand old mansions of Bank Street, where formal dinner parties had been a regular occurrence.

As one might imagine, these meals were not my favorite pastime. My father insisted that I take the first seat on the side, next to his at the head of the long table, where he would murmur under his breath things like, "David, shift your knife when you cut your meat," or "David, don't take such big bites," or "David, eat everything on your plate." On the last, he was a stickler, and not just at dinner but at all meals.

And the students knew it. They were constantly playing jokes on me, and perhaps the most devilish of all took advantage of my notorious weakness for ice cream. I came home from school for lunch and customarily got home around noon, with lunch occurring promptly at 12:30. One day, two of the students, Freddy Francis and Harold Hodgins, called me up to their room and asked me to help them. "Look, David, we got a couple of half-gallons of chocolate ice cream this morning, and we've eaten one and thrown the container away, but now we've got to get rid of this second half-gallon before lunch, or it will melt and we'll get caught. The trouble is we can't eat any more; you've got to help us," they pleaded.

How could I refuse? So I sat down, took the spoon they offered me, and dutifully went to work. I hastily scooped up the last bite, just as we heard the others going down to the dining room for lunch.

"Oh, thanks, David, you really saved our bacon," Freddy said, stuffing the empty carton under the bed, and I nodded, thinking it odd that Harold seemed to be convulsed with laughter or something. I thought he probably felt a bit ill from having eaten too much ice cream. Come to think of it, I wasn't feeling so well myself. In fact, I was decidedly bloated, as my eyes caught up with my distended stomach. The last thing I wanted was a hearty meal, but it was a little late to think of that now.

We got to our places at the table just as my father bowed his head for grace. When we sat down at lunch that day, my eyes began to glaze slightly at the sight of the size of the portions my father was heaping on my plate. He paused with the last spoonful of carrots in midair, because down the table Freddy and Harold had their hands over their mouths, quaking with laughter, and I began to realize I had been had. "Francis? Hodgins? Is anything the matter?" my father inquired.

"Oh, no, sir," Freddy managed to reply. "Harold just told me a joke, um, about some ice cream," and with that he and Harold broke up, trying so hard to keep their laughter in. By this time, the other students knew something was up and were picking up the mirth, and my father wisely gave them a loose rein. "Well," he said, smiling, "unless it is something you can share with the rest of us, you'd better keep it to yourselves. The dining table is not the place for nonsense or horseplay."

"Yes, sir," Freddy hastily agreed, carefully avoiding looking in my direction.

In the meantime, I had grown somewhat ashen, for there was another rule at the dinner table: the meal was not concluded until everyone was finished, and then we closed in prayer. With attention paid throughout to correct table manners and proper decorum, it was really a formal affair, even at lunch when we didn't have to wear coats and ties. I stared forlornly at the pile of food on my plate. No longer hot, bits of grease were beginning to congeal at the edges of the corned beef, and the boiled potatoes were looking increasingly glutinous. Worst of all, I could still taste chocolate ice cream, and the aftertaste of it was decidedly unpleasant.

And then it came, the murmur to my right that I had been dreading: "Eat up your plate, David." Down both sides of the long table came the muffled sound of choked off laughter, and I surmised that Freddy and Harold had somehow let the story out. I looked up and glared in their direction—and was shocked to see the suggestion of a smile playing at the corner of my own mother's lips. Would they have dared tell her? Probably not, but she herself had an irrepressible sense of humor and had no doubt guessed in general what was going on. It wasn't too hard, since I normally ate like a farmhand.

Well, I would show them all! And I began to eat, grim determination steeling my innards. Somehow I got it all in, right down to the last cold carrot. And when dessert was finally offered, I politely declined, and everyone burst out laughing, a bit of improper decorum which my father chose to ignore.

That sort of thing happened to me all the time at Annesley, and it was as if I had suddenly inherited thirty mischievous older brothers—whom

I dearly loved except at those moments when I was the butt of their practical jokes. Those were character-building years for me as well as for the students.

In the evenings, dad would read to us, not from the Bible, but from the classics of Christian literature, which happily included some of the modern classics, like *The Robe* and *Quo Vadis*. Here, in these evening sessions in the spacious living room with a fire crackling in the big hearth, was the one place, other than the pulpit, in which my father felt it was permissible to give full vent to his emotions. He would get so involved in the stories he was reading, that they would come alive for us, and at particularly poignant passages, he might even be moved to tears. Many of those stories made a lasting impression on me, because I could see the events happening as dad read.

We also listened to the radio occasionally, to mystery programs like "The Shadow Knows" and "Inner Sanctum," but I sensed that my father felt their moral content was somewhat suspect, and that one of the reasons he read in the evenings was to provide an alternate source of entertainment. And I must say that when I finally did see one of the early television sets a few years later, the dramas did not have nearly the suspense and impact of the books my father had read aloud.

After reading, we were free to chat or write letters or putter around, but ten o'clock was still ten o'clock in my father's book. And if any of the students were out, well, they knew the rule. I have a mental picture of my father standing by the front door, pocket watch in hand. I'll never forget the evening that Jim Poynter was coming up the walk just at ten. Jim had recently gotten out of the army, and mother was not too sure of his Christian testimony, so she asked Marian Clow to "keep an eye on him." (They wound up getting married and are both working at 100 Huntley Street now.) On the night in question, Jim was halfway up the walk when dad closed the door and locked it and pulled down the shade. Jim had to find somewhere else to stay that night, and needless to say, it never happened again.

On Sundays, we went to the Fifth Avenue Holiness Church, which was pastored by my mother's brother, Manley Pritchard, and which was the largest in our denomination. I liked Uncle Manley, but I did an awful lot of sleeping during his sermons. Fortunately, I was still young enough to get away with it; once a body got to be high school age, he was expected to concentrate on the sermon, and I could see the older boys painfully learning the art of "resting their eyes" or "meditating in an attitude of prayer" as they drank in the priceless pearls.

For us youngsters, there were one or two old characters, as in Ramsayville, who could be counted on for blessed diversion. Mr. Gough was an eighty-year-old retired preacher who had in his day started several churches and was well respected. No one would ever dream of saying anything to him that might offend him. But he did have a habit of falling asleep, and he, too, was of an age where this was not looked upon askance. Unfortunately (or fortunately, depending upon where you were on the age scale), he also had a habit of waking up with a start and crying out, "Amen!" Perhaps he was embarrassed at having dozed off and wanted to show that he was involved with what was going on; the trouble was, his loud contribution always came at a singularly inappropriate time, and I suspected that Uncle Manley and other preachers must have regarded him as if he were a ticking time bomb. When he did go off, all the children in church would burst into laughter, and hearing this, he would mistake it for the sound of people getting blessed, and so, pleased with himself for having awakened right in the middle of a spontaneous celebration, he would shout, "Amen, amen." This, of course, provoked even more hilarity, much to the dismay of the good ladies of the church.

Sunday afternoons were still considered to be mandatory rest periods, but there was no river to go by for a walk, and since I could not sit still all afternoon, my parents said it would be all right for me to go to other Sunday schools. Right after lunch, I would get on my bike and head for the two o'clock Sunday school at the Gospel Tabernacle, a Christian and Missionary Alliance church, and then at five minutes to three, I would slip out in time to make the three o'clock Sunday school at the Salvation Army. It is hard to imagine a young person wanting to go to three hours of Sunday school, but there was nothing else to do, and I grew to enjoy them.

The years passed swiftly in Ottawa, and suddenly they came to an end. Nowadays, you hear a great deal about church splits and schisms and division in the body of Christ, but it wasn't always that way. Thirty years ago, there were such things as church unions, and my father helped engineer one. For a long time, our denomination had felt a kindred spirit with other holiness churches in our area, and the Brockville Bible College paralleled the work and purpose of Annesley College, while at the same time having a certified high school, as well as a seminary. After working at it for a year, my father helped negotiate a union between the two, which he hoped would be a forerunner of the joining together of the two denominations. The success of his accomplishment, however, left him abruptly out of a job.

And so, he went back to what was really his first love in Canada: pastoring. He was offered the job of pastoring a circuit made up of two small churches in Haley's Station and Admaston, villages near Renfrew in the Ottawa Valley, about seventy miles northwest of the capital. We moved there in September, 1948, and I was back in a one-room schoolhouse, this time as an eighth-grader, learning the things on which I had eavesdropped many years before. My teacher was Miss Lydia Conners and she was able to inspire in me a real interest in geometry, as well as social studies. It was a good year, though it was marred by tragedy—the first tragedy I ever had to walk through, and one that would leave a scar for the rest of my life.

CHAPTER 4

King of the Road

Not long after we moved to Haley's Station in the late summer of 1948, mother began to complain of abdominal pains. She admitted she had been having them back at Annesley, but she had been too busy with her work there to pay any attention to them. Now they had grown so severe that it was impossible to ignore them, so dad took her to the hospital at Renfrew. They told him she had an inflammation in her uterus and recommended bed rest, which frustrated mother, since she had begun making calls as the pastor's wife, and had several couples in town who did not know the Lord very much on her heart. Mother was the gentlest evangelist I have ever known. She did not have to say much, for Jesus fairly shone through her when she spoke of Him. After a few visits, people just began coming to church and eventually to Christ.

The pains grew more severe, so dad took her back to the hospital. During the week she was there, her condition continued to worsen, and finally they recommended that she go to Ottawa Civic Hospital. There it was discovered that she had cancer of the womb, and that the cancer was in an advanced stage. Cobalt radiation and chemotherapy were not in use in those days; the only effective treatment was major surgery in the earliest stages. Although my sisters and I were not told at the time, mother's cancer had progressed far beyond the possibility of surgery.

We celebrated Christmas that year in her hospital room. Mother had had her hair done and was propped up in bed with a new bed jacket. She was as cheerful as if she were home and nothing were the matter. She really looked good. We opened our presents, and dad read from the second chapter of Luke, as he did every Christmas. It was a blessed Christmas, and while we were with her, we were genuinely able to banish any forebodings we may have had.

On Sunday afternoon, the seventeenth of January, the call came for dad to come to the hospital as quickly as possible and to bring the children. Father drove our new Chevrolet as fast as he dared over the treacherous, icy roads. Mother was still alive when we got to her room, and it was obvious that the nurses had been doing their best to keep her there until we arrived. As soon as we stepped into the room, they took their instruments and departed.

When we were gathered around her bed, all of us in tears, mother looked from one to another, and then her gaze rested on me, and she tried to speak. I thought her lips formed my name, and I went to her side. And then I said something that surprised me: "I'll meet you in heaven, mother. I will!" She smiled and sighed and was gone.

I was inconsolable for several days. The person I loved most in the world, who had been both mother and father to me for half my life had been taken from me. But three things penetrated my grief: first, the fact that mother was now in heaven made that place tangible to me. Heaven was now a reality for me, because she was there. Secondly, my father's own deep grief so touched me that in those three days of preparing for the funeral, we grew closer than we had ever been before. "If ever there was a saint of God," he told me, "it was your mother. In all the twenty-four years we were married, I never heard her say an unkind word." And I realized somehow that the highest mark of respect that dad could pay her was to say that to me.

The third thing was a miracle—the first supernatural experience of my life. On the Sunday after the funeral, Bob Code and his wife came to the Haley church for the first time, and dad was pleased to see them, because they had been the couple most on mother's heart. Bob Code had a strange story to tell. The previous Sunday evening, he and his wife were at home reading when my mother appeared and pleaded with them to give their lives to the Lord. And then, as abruptly as she had come, she vanished. Bob and his wife had been badly shaken, and all week long they had tried to put it out of mind but couldn't, and so they had come to church.

"What time did this occur, Mr. Code?" my dad asked.

"I don't know; it must have been around 7:30. Why?"

"Because Hazel passed away last Sunday—around 7:30."

Bob and his wife thought about that, and decided to give their lives to

Christ. And I sensed that mother was watching up in heaven with her beautiful smile. I also sensed she was looking at me—to see when I would give *my* life to the Lord. But I was not quite ready.

Life was comparatively bleak for the next few years. Father did his best to look after us and provide all the care we needed, just as mother had during the war when he was in Egypt. We appreciated his efforts on our behalf, and tried to carry on as if nothing had changed, doing our best to help fill the gaping hole in his own heart. After a year or so, we began to gently kid him about whom he might take for a wife, for we all felt that he should remarry. There was a loneliness in his life, and it even showed up in his preaching. The two churches were growing, and souls were being saved. But there was not the excitement and the joy that had so thrilled dad in previous years. From the pulpit, he would tell of Egyptian congregations getting up out of their pews and dancing for joy, of blind Bakeeta, and many other stories. He would become elated as he preached about those things, and sometimes he would weep, but his congregations would just sit there, untouched.

I believed the stories. In my mind, I could see the things happening that he described, and I felt the first vague yearning to experience them myself. But it soon passed, and I would settle back into the torpor of another Sunday. I sensed that dad privately missed the intensity of the interaction with the Lord that he experienced in Egypt, and that he longed to go back. I used to imagine what it would be like to go with him, to carry his baggage and help set up meetings for him.

Two years after mother's death, my sister Elaine married an American named Glen Thompson from Buffalo, and a few months later, Willa got engaged to Harold Hodgins of Pembroke, one of the Annesley students who had played the ice cream joke on me. Soon there would be only dad and me, and we were all glad when he began to take an interest in Elva Bishop, whose mother had been an evangelist and whose father had been one of the great preachers in the Holiness Movement. She herself was a live wire and a doer, and her specialty was raising funds for missionary work, which endeared her to dad all the more. They were married on September 10, 1951, just after I, their best man, had turned fifteen.

Almost immediately, they left for the mission field, my father having now been made superintendent of all the work in Egypt. They left their best man behind. Instead, I became a grade-eleven boarder at the

Brockville Bible College. In my head, I accepted the rational explanation: there was no decent education to be had for English-speaking high school students in Egypt. The political situation was again unsettled, with the British presence in the Suez Canal zone becoming an increasing irritant to the nationalistic Egyptians. And missionary children traditionally went to boarding schools at home to complete their education, while their parents were abroad.

But in my heart I felt abandoned. I felt the world had dealt me a raw deal, and I dreamed of saving enough money to buy passage to Egypt and just show up, unannounced on my father's doorstep. He'd *have* to take me in then! But my savings would have to be built up from scratch, for I had just taken the considerable sum of money I had saved over the years and blown it all on a motorcycle—a 198c.c.,burgundy-colored, British James.

Getting a license a year ahead of the customary age was not easy, but in those days, they had people instead of computers in the provincial license bureau, and I was able to persuade them to give me a restricted license just for the motorcycle, so that I could visit my sisters, each of whom lived two hundred miles from me. And so, I spent as much of the weekends as I could cruising. I was allowed to be away for the weekend, visiting my sisters or other distant relatives, providing I let them know where I was going.

What, in fact, I did was join a motorcycle club in Kingston, called "The Throttle Twisters." Back in the early fifties, motorcycle clubs did not have the connotation they have subsequently gained; they were more like amateur sports car clubs are today. We were a group of enthusiasts who would organize off-the-trail gymkhanas, where we would time ourselves over difficult courses in the bush, and see if we could get through without spilling or putting a foot down.

But in spite of all the riding, there was a hollowness in me that no long-distance cruising seemed to fill. I would think nothing of riding from Toronto to Ottawa, a five-hour trip. At least, when I was riding, there was always the possibility that things might be better at my destination, wherever that happened to be. Of course, they weren't, but as long as I was en route, I could at least maintain the illusion that they might be.

But all trips must come to an end, and Monday morning would find me back in Brockville Bible College, walking down the same old corridor to my first class. One of the portraits in that corridor was of the founder of the Holiness Movement, the legendary R.C. Horner. If no one else was in sight when I went by, I would turn his picture around and leave him facing the wall. I did so many things like that that I gained a reputation for having a real chip on my shoulder.

And one Wednesday night, I capped it. I had taken up the trumpet in grade six, and by grade eleven I was playing well enough to be invited to play in the Salvation Army band. That got me out on Wednesday nights to practice, only on the Wednesday night in question band practice was canceled, so I decided to take in the neighborhood movie. It was just my luck that that night the principal happened to be driving downtown and noticed my motorcycle parked in front of the Odeon Theatre. When I arrived back, he called me into his office and confronted me point-blank; I couldn't lie, and that was the end of my getting out on Wednesday nights.

At the same time that I was in the height of my rebellion, I was being forced to take stock of some pretty far-reaching alternatives. I had a part-time job at a service station as a pump-jockey and general handyman. The men who hung around that place used the foulest language I had ever heard, drinking and smoking and maligning all women with filthy humor. I could not help but compare that life style with my parents', and I knew I didn't want to come into adulthood and live that way. Yet, on the other hand, I still wasn't ready to make any kind of no-strings-attached commitment to Christ, either. And so there I was, turning slowly over a slow fire.

The fire heated up a bit when, at the end of the school year, the principal informed me that I was not welcome to come back for grade twelve. My father, embarrassed and deeply disappointed in me, arranged for me to board with my sister Willa and her husband, Harold, in Pembroke and finish high school there. But I was not about to go directly to Pembroke and trade one regime of discipline for another. I had other plans for that summer—and for at least a year thereafter.

Putting an ad in the paper to sell my beloved motorcycle, I went down to Montreal, and there I spent day after day on the docks, trying to talk one Mediterranean-bound skipper after another into signing me on as a deck hand so I could work my way across to Egypt. I had already ascertained that even if I were able to sell my bike for a decent price (which I wasn't), it would not be enough to book passage on a steamship. But I was too young and could not get into the seamen's union, and so, completely frustrated, I gave up and went back to Pembroke.

As soon as I got there, I went job-hunting and quickly landed a job as a handyman at the Chrysler dealership there. I saved up enough money to trade in my James 198c.c. on a huge, pre-war Harley Davidson 74, which in 1952 was the biggest road machine then made. No more off-the-trail stuff for me; that hog could do better than a hundred on the straightaway. And of course, I now had the leather jacket and the kidney belt and the half-Wellington boots to go with it. We didn't wear helmets in those days; I rode bareheaded, but I had a white silk scarf which I let whip out behind me. As the pop hit declared, I was the "King of the Road," for sure!

In the meantime, circumstances also seemed to be piling up on the other side of the scale. It turned out that my boss, Sid Healey, was an evangelizing Baptist, and Warren Schizkoskie, the head of the parts department, where I would continue working after school, was a Pentecostal. All summer long, Sid never missed a chance to witness to me, and he really gave me the gospel, straight on. And in his own way, Warren did too, though he was more soft-sell, telling me of the sweetness and the light and the abiding joy of living in Jesus. With the two of them double-teaming me, it was a wonder I was able to hold out at all.

The biggest charge I got out of working at Sid's was at the end of the summer when he would occasionally let me take out his big Chrysler on an errand. I was sixteen by then, and had gotten not just an operator's license, but a chauffeur's license, so I could drive the service department's tow truck. But the thing I liked most was to get behind the wheel of that long blue Chrysler. And Sid knew it. So one day, shortly before the beginning of school, he asked me if I would mind driving a bunch of young people from his church down to Jack Wyrtzen's Word of Life Camp on Schroon Lake, New York, for a weekend gathering. I jumped at the chance—as he knew I would.

I was determined I wasn't going to be hustled into any kind of lifetime commitment, and of course, wouldn't you know, no one tried. We just had a good time—they were a kind, wonderful bunch of kids—and I was particularly impressed with Gil Dodds, the indoor-mile champion who was the camp's activities director, who *lived* the Christian life, rather than talking about it.

I was still unsaved when we returned to Pembroke, but I had been given a lot to think about. And though I didn't know it, my time was a lot shorter than I realized.

CHAPTER 5

No Strings Attached

When school started in the fall of '52, I was sixteen, six-foot-one-inch tall, and weighed 185, and in those days there wasn't an unnecessary ounce or inch on me. I thought I was pretty tough, and so I went out for the football team. Although I was a junior, I made the seniors' team, playing right tackle. My favorite thing was to bang through the opponents' line and see if I could tackle the ball carrier. To play football well, you really have to enjoy hitting, and I delighted in the impact.

We played a rough game but a clean one. The only time I got into a fight was when we were playing against Renfrew in a close game, and I felt someone give me the knee. I grabbed the fellow I thought it was and hauled off and decked him, and got ejected from the game. But except for that incident, my latent hostility was confined to the approved outlets of the game.

So I had football and my motorcycle and my fierce independence—and for the most part, I was miserable. It began to dawn on me that even if I would be able to get over to Egypt and be with my father, that that would not necessarily fill the void. It seemed to be something that was just in me, a hollowness that would always be there.

Of course, Sid and Warren, down at the dealership where I worked after school, were sure they had the answer. If only I would turn my life over to the Lord— But during the last couple of years, without my mother and with my father away, I had grown used to doing what I wanted and going where I wanted, when I wanted to, with no one to tell me what to do. And unhappy though I was, I wasn't sure I wanted to change my way of living. I liked my independence.

Yet now, in addition to Sid and Warren, it turned out that four of the ten guys in my Latin class (I had always liked Latin for some reason) were committed Christians—three Pentecostals and a Baptist. And they had the courage of their convictions; they never hesitated to speak up even when popular opinion in the classroom was running counter to their position, or a teacher put down their beliefs. I grudgingly began to admire them.

I started watching them that fall, looking for the one instance of hypocrisy which would put the lie to the things they were saying. But they never seemed to slip, and the more closely I observed their life style the more it seemed to conform with a life style whose consistency I had already experienced—my parents'.

They were regular guys. I played football with a couple of them, and one, Wally Johnson, had a perfect gem of a '34 Ford which we did some double-dating in. The four of us seemed to grow fairly close, and they too began to encourage me to "seek the Lord," as they said in those days. One evening, the three Pentecostals took me and a couple of other fellows to a special youth service at their church. We nonbelievers sat in the back, with our friends alongside, and we made fun of the service in a running commentary of snide remarks. I joined in and felt badly doing so, but I didn't want any of them to think I was being taken in.

And then, during the singing of the chorus, "Jesus is the Sweetest Name I Know," I happened to look over at Wally, and I thought I saw what looked like tears glimmering in his eyes. In that instant, in my heart I knew that what they had found was reality, that they were genuine, and that what they were feeling was real. The mockery quieted down after that, and later that night, after we had dropped the others off, Wally and I sat in his '34 Ford, and talked until well after midnight.

Not long after that, Sid Healey invited me to Ottawa to hear Jack Wyrtzen at a Youth for Christ rally, saying that his eyes were not up to the driving, and asked if I would drive for him. I was delighted, not just for the opportunity to drive the Chrysler, but because I had long enjoyed listening to Jack Wyrtzen's "Word of Life Hour" on Sunday afternoons. Also present at the rally, as one of the singers, was Homer James, who had been a couple of years ahead of me at Brockville (and who is now a singer in the Billy Graham team). Jack invited all who would like to give their lives to Christ to come forward. Homer came down off the platform to where I stood and put his arm around me. "David," he said gently, "don't you plan sometime to give your heart to God?"

"Yes, I do intend to, Homer," I replied and realized that was the first time I had ever said so.

"Doesn't it make sense that you should do it tonight?" he asked gently, and all of a sudden, it did make sense, a lot of sense.

I went forward. A man I didn't know and whose name I never learned quoted this Bible verse to me. "Him that cometh to me I will in no wise cast out" (John 6:37). I had heard it many times before, but suddenly I was hearing it as if for the first time. I had just come forward to Jesus, and He said that He would not cast me out. Therefore, He must take me in; indeed He *has* taken me in. I am His, and He is mine. Suddenly I *knew* that the transaction had taken place.

I told the man who was ministering to me what I had seen, and, smiling broadly, he led me in a prayer: "Here I am, Lord Jesus; I thank you that you keep your word. You said that you would take me in, and I thank you now for having taken me in, for forgiving me all of my sin, and for washing it away in the blood which you shed on the cross. Thank you, Lord Jesus. Amen."

As we parted, that man gave me four things to do which, he said, if I were faithful to them, would help keep me centered in the Christian life: (1) Read your Bible every day—and give God a chance to speak to you through His Word; (2) Have a time of prayer every day, when *you* talk to God; (3) Share your faith with someone else regularly; and (4) Get into a church where you will have good teaching and fellowship with others who know and love the Lord too. As I was to find out, those four things are right on.

The following afternoon, I knew I had to do something, and it filled my heart with anxiety. It was December, football was over, and the basketball team had begun to practice for the coming season. I was on the team, and as we gathered in the locker room and got ready for the afternoon's workout, I said, "Hey, you guys, can I have your attention for a minute? I've got something to tell you." The locker room quieted down, and the guys turned to me in curious attention. For a moment, I wished I'd never opened my mouth, but forced myself to go on. "Last night, in Ottawa, at a Youth for Christ rally, I went forward and gave my life to Christ. For me, it's going to be a new ball game from now on."

There were a few kidding cheers, and jokes like: "Hey, get that: Mainse has got religion!" But as the days went on, and they saw I meant business, their attitude changed to one of respect, and I found I did not lose any of the friends I really cared about as I had feared I might. My own heart attitude changed too; in fact, I was surprised at how quickly some of my character traits fell away. Almost immediately, for example, my language began to clean up, and within a couple of weeks I had shed much of the cynicism in which I had couched so much of what I said or thought, and with which I had led others in a negative direction. At the same time, I began to spend more and more time with the three fellows who were Pentecostals, going to their church and being invited to their homes. I often talked with Wally into the night as we sat together in his Ford.

One of the first things I did was write to my father in Egypt and tell him what had happened to me. Our denomination's missionary outreach to Egypt had been under persecution the past year, because Canada was a member of the British Commonwealth, and Britain was now coming under heavy attack. The British essentially ruled Egypt under the same mandate with which they had ruled Palestine, after defeating Turkey in World War I, and to do so, they maintained King Farouk as a puppet head of state. But in July, a young colonel named Nasser had led an army revolt which had deposed Farouk and established General Naguib as head of state. Feelings against the British were running high.

My father bore the brunt of this personally. Like the rest of our missionaries, the locals assumed they were British, and it was a common occurrence to have slogans like "British dogs, we will kill you" painted on the wide doors of his mission's garage. Some of his pastors had been stoned and their church windows broken, so dad demanded a meeting with General Naguib. He was received and was given wonderful promises, but nothing tangible came to pass, and it became obvious that nothing ever would. Depressed and discouraged, yet driving himself harder than ever to preach and win more souls for Christ, my father suffered a massive heart attack in November, 1952, which left him bedridden for several months.

Knowing how it would cheer him, especially after all the bad news he had been receiving about me, I wrote him a glowing report of my conversion. I told him of my new friends, and the fellowship we were having, and how my attitude about everything had changed. And indeed, he was as pleased as I had hoped he would be—except about one thing. "I want you to stay away from Pentecostal churches. There are plenty of churches within our own denomination where you can find fellowship."

I was crushed. I wanted to be obedient to my father, but my first obedience had to be to God, and I had felt His clear leading in the direction I was taking. And I began to remember a few other things: on several occasions, my mother had taken me to the Bethel Pentecostal Church in Ottawa for some special meetings and while I sensed that there was something not quite acceptable about the Pentecostals which was never spelled out, still she had taken me.

I also recalled her telling me about Lillian Trasher, the most famous missionary in Egypt, who had lived in the same city as she and my father. Lillian had founded an orphanage entirely on faith and had seen it grow to the place where it sheltered more than two thousand orphans, plus many mothers who had been abandoned, for in the Moslem religion, all a husband has to do is say "I divorce you" four times, and that's the end of it—no support, no alimony, nothing. Lillian had taken these people in as well, and in my mother's eyes, she was pretty close to a living saint.

So, despite my father's admonition, I continued to fellowship with my Pentecostal friends. And now my conversations with Wally began to turn to the topic of speaking in tongues. Wally directed me to Acts 2, 10 and 19, to what happened in the lives of Paul and the other apostles. I saw that Jesus had promised His disciples He would send the Holy Spirit to take His place, and that the Spirit would not just dwell with them, as He had, but *within* them. I saw where Peter explained what had happened on the day of Pentecost by quoting Joel 2, where God promised to pour out His Spirit on all flesh. I saw in Acts 8, where Peter and John prayed for the recently converted Samaritans to be filled with the Holy Spirit. And so on.

Gradually, after much study and prayer, I became convinced I needed this dimension in my Christian experience, and so I began to pray for it. But, because I knew what the reaction in my denomination would be, I always added, "But please, Lord, no speaking in tongues." And the more I prayed, the hungrier I became for all that God had for me.

In March, my father's condition had not improved, and his doctors decided that the only thing left to do was to send him back to Canada, to the climate and food he had always known. And so, my father was flown home, with Elva at his side, and his nephew, Lorne Kenny, assisting him. My sister and I were at the airport when he landed in Ottawa. He had to be helped off the plane, and he was shockingly thin and pale. I wanted to rush up and hug him and tell him how much I loved him, but because of the reserve that was still there, we did little more than shake hands. Then dad was taken away to the convalescent home where he would spend the next two months building up his strength.

In the meantime, my own hunger for the fullness of the Holy Spirit and all that God had for me continued to grow until, around the beginning of June, I could stand it no longer. The breakthrough came on a Thursday evening when I was home studying for my final departmental Latin exam in the morning. I got a strong urge to go over to church where there was a meeting with a visiting evangelist. I was torn, because I knew I needed to study for that exam, as it was being given not by the local school board, but by the Department of Education in Toronto, and I had goofed off the year before in Brockville. Yet all I could think about was that meeting over at church.

Finally, I stopped fighting it and got on my motorcycle and rode into town. I got there in time for the end of the evangelist's message, and when he gave the invitation for those who wanted to be prayed for to receive the baptism in the Holy Spirit, I was one of the first into the prayer room and down on my knees. "God," I cried, "I want *all* that I can take at this time, and I don't care if I never get off my knees." I was actually on my knees only about five minutes, when something happened to me that had never happened before. The power of God came upon me from the top of my head to the tips of my toes, and it forced me to the floor, so that I couldn't move a muscle.

And the Lord seemed to be speaking to me: *Do you believe this is my power?*

"Yes, Lord," I thought, "I know it's your power, and I want to be filled with your Spirit, but, please, Lord, no tongues."

David, are you willing to believe that as I fill you with the Spirit, you will speak in tongues as the Spirit gives you utterance, even as my disciples did on the day of Pentecost?

"All right, Lord, *that* I'll accept, but I don't want anything less than they got on that day." And with that, I surrendered completely to God, no strings attached.

Although I still couldn't move, I felt a tingling all over my body, a not unpleasant sensation of the flesh being warmed. Then suddenly I regained the movement of my hands and feet. My mouth was released at the same time, and I burst out in tongues—a heavenly prayer language which I could not understand, but which somehow seemed to perfectly express the overflowing joy I felt in my heart. I was so happy deep inside that I jumped up and danced around the prayer room, and gave Pastor George Bombay a great bear hug, which took his breath away.

Then, overjoyed, I said goodbye and went outside to my motorcycle, intending to go home and study. As I rode through the night, my hands were up in the air praising God more than they were on the handlebars. I had just memorized the words of "How Great Thou Art," and now I sang them at the top of my lungs, gazing up at the stars, and only occasionally remembering to keep an eye out for traffic. I was drunk on new wine, and I didn't care if the whole world knew it. When I got to my sister's house, I kept right on singing out on the porch, though not as loudly, and the Spirit of God fell upon me again. I must have stayed out there for two hours, worshiping God and praising Him in the new language He had given me, until finally I wound down a little. It was after one o'clock before I went in and got into bed. Four hours later, I was up and as wide awake and refreshed as if I had been sleeping all night. I studied for an hour, then went to school and passed the Latin exam with flying colors.

Also, in June, my father was reappointed to the two churches in Haley's Station and Admaston which he had pastored before going to Egypt, his replacement having coincidentally been called elsewhere just when he returned. Dad was deeply pleased, for he had grown to love these two congregations, and he and Elva and I moved into the same parsonage in which we had lived before.

I did not tell him I had spoken in tongues; it was all so new to me, I stopped using my prayer language after that first night. At first, I was afraid God might force the issue, or be displeased with me for not using the gift which He had given me, but neither proved to be the case. Dad got settled in smoothly, and was beginning to receive callers—the doctors felt it would not be wise for him to start preaching right away—and he was as happy as he had been before mother died. It looked like we were heading into the first good summer we had had in years.

And then I heard from Wally Johnson that his older brother Bob was about to pioneer a church that summer down in Madoc, and Wally said he needed any help he could get. I yearned to join Bob, to play the trumpet in the streets with them, and to be a part of the new work that God was about to raise up in the town I used to live in.

I went down to my father's room and told him about it, and that I wanted to go. He knew it would be a Pentecostal church, and his reply was short and to the point: "If you go, you are going against my will!"

CHAPTER 6

The Call

I left my father quickly, so he wouldn't see how crushed I was, and I went up to my room and shut the door. Kneeling by my bed, I poured out my heart to God—and in the midst of my despair, His Spirit once again descended on me, as it had a month before. My prayer language again flowed. Getting my Bible from the bedside table, I held it in my hand and said, "Lord, I believe you want me to help Bob on the streets in Madoc, and my father has said no—what should I do?" And in desperation, I let the Bible fall open and looked down. My eye fell on "Blow ye the trumpet in the land" (Jer. 4:5).

Elated, and feeling the strong presence of the Holy Spirit all about me, I went back downstairs to talk to my father. It was a good half hour past ten o'clock, but I was counting on his not being asleep yet, and he wasn't.

I knew if I hesitated, I'd never say it, so I blurted it right out: "I know you will not be pleased to hear this, but I have spoken in tongues. It happened about a month ago back in Pembroke, and I haven't done it since—until just now." I rushed on, before he could speak. "The power of God is on me to say this to you right now, and I want you to know I love you, and I respect you, and I care for you. But I've asked my heavenly Father what I should do, and I let the Bible fall open, and here is what it fell open to," and I read him the verse from Jeremiah. I said, "I believe that refers to my own trumpet, and that God is telling me to go." I looked at him, hoping that he would see it that way too.

But he didn't. With voice filled with sadness, he said, "Well, I won't stand in your way—you can go." And with that, the subject was closed.

I went down to Madoc and joined Bob, sleeping on the floor of the little apartment he was renting, and "blowing the trumpet in the land" at every opportunity. We held street meetings in the middle of town; in fact, the owner of the hotel complained to the village council that our meetings across the street from his hotel were ruining his business.

Those weekends of working with Bob were the most fulfilling of my life up to then, and his dedication had a profound effect on me. He would get up early in the morning and would pray for an hour or two without stopping, and there was never the slightest doubt in his mind that he would spend the rest of his life serving the Lord. (And so he is, with an open-line ministry in Montreal and a church he co-pastors with his brother Wally.)

As a result of Bob's influence, and the influence of my father's life, I began to seek the Lord, to see if He might call me into the ministry. "Lord, I would love it if you were to call me. But I know from my dad's experience that if there is anything else I can do in life, when the going gets tough, I might fall back on that. So I don't want to go into the ministry, unless I am sure it's the *only* thing you want me to do." Over and over, I prayed in this fashion, waiting for the Holy Spirit's whisper, and frustrated that it didn't come right away.

In August, just before my seventeenth birthday, Bob took me to a youth camp at Cobourg, to hear an evangelist from Florida. By this time my prayer had become, "Lord, please grant me the privilege of being in your service," for all I wanted now was to be as close to Him as I could.

There were more than a thousand young people there that night, and after the meeting was over, the majority of the young people went forward for prayer around the altars. A group of ministers joined the evangelist, and they began to move through the tabernacle, laying on hands and praying. When the evangelist got to me, all of a sudden, he began to prophesy, *"You are called into the ministry of the Lord Jesus Christ. This is the work God has set you apart for, and you will never be able to do anything else."*

I was stunned; I had not told anyone of my prayer, not even Bob. But from that point on, I knew absolutely that I was called to ministry. This time, I did not spring this revelation on my father right away, but let it simmer throughout the summer. One of the two industries near Haley's Station was the light alloys plant about four miles from the station, and I got a summer job there. The plant was making Orenda jet engines, and I got a job as a fetler, which meant I would carefully grind the rough edges off of the fresh metal castings.

Once I had learned the job's routine, it did not take a lot of concentration, and the machinery we worked around was so loud that I was able to sing choruses, and even speak in tongues. The other workers thought I was simply singing to myself and paid no attention, so day after day I would be continually blessed while I worked. On top of that, during our lunch break, the Lord allowed me to lead my first soul to Jesus Christ—one of the workers on the assembly line. I was so overjoyed I could have exploded, and told Bob about it that weekend, for I was still spending each weekend in Madoc, continuing to help him pioneer the little church.

The next opportunity I had to do His work on my own was with the young people's group my father had allowed me to start in the Haley's Station church. Rounding up all the young people I could find, a good carload, I took them down to Ottawa, to hear Hyman Appleman, the Jewish evangelist. That night, every one of them gave their lives to the Lord, and they became the nucleus of an enthusiastic young people's group in Haley's Station. The town really needed one; the main excitement of an evening was to watch the 7:03 come in. The station was in the centre of town—indeed, it *was* the centre, hence the town's name—and we would watch the mail be dropped off. Then we watched as it was taken to the general store and sorted by Mr. Howard, after which we picked up any mail that had come for our families and went home and played kick-the-can, or else hung around the general store, sitting on nail kegs or what-have-you. Yes, there was a definite need for a young Christian group in Haley's Station.

Grade thirteen promised to be my most difficult and challenging year. I was glad that Ontario had an optional extra grade at the end of high school, because I felt I needed the intellectual discipline. That in itself was a miracle, considering what my attitude had been the year before, before I had come to the Lord. But grade thirteen was tough, the equivalent of freshman year at college. Only five of the students successfully completed it in one year, and I was one of the five.

I also went out for football again, and the first thing I did was look up the fellow I had slugged the year before when I had been playing against Renfrew, and I asked him to forgive me. He did so without hesitation. In fact, I let all the guys know where I stood and they respected my stand for the Lord. I played the game hard but clean, and I loved every minute. If anything took too much precedence in my life and threatened to crowd Jesus out of the center, it was sports. The Lord had also given me the coordination to play basketball and baseball, but my favorite sport of all was track and field, especially the shot put. I won that event in the annual Ottawa Valley track meet and set an intermediate record that stood for a number of years.

My one disappointment in sports was that my father never went to a game or meet in which I participated. He had been in sports. He even had a broken nose from playing hockey, and every finger of his left hand had swollen knuckles from being a catcher back in the days when they played hardball with unpadded gloves. But when he had gone into the ministry, he had set aside all further interest in sports as being unsuitable for a man of God, and a very carnal pastime. Nevertheless, he would glory in those old days, when I would get him to tell me about them, and how I longed for him to just once come out and throw the ball around with me.

As the fall of '53 progressed and our young people's group grew, I finally shared with my father the feeling I had that God was calling me into the ministry. His enthusiasm at this news was somewhat modulated, and I was sure it was because of the subject which neither of us had raised since that night in July—the baptism in the Holy Spirit and tongues. But one of the senior preachers of our denomination was passing through town at that time, and my father suggested I have a talk with him.

The preacher laid it on the line: "If you are ever going to be a Holiness minister, you're going to have to remain absolutely silent about the tongues experience."

"But if it *was* God—" I started to object, but he raised his hand.

"There's nothing to be gained in arguing that point with you, since you are obviously convinced that it was. I'm just saying that you will never be able to preach or share about it, and will have to regard it as if it never happened."

What he had to say left me in deep anguish. I knew I was called to the ministry, and I assumed I would follow the family tradition and that it would be in the Holiness Movement. It had never occurred to me that I might one day be associated with the Pentecostal Assemblies of Canada, even though I had received the baptism in one of their churches.

Yet I had seen what had happened in my own family when I had told my father and stepmother, Elva, about my experience, and I could imagine their response magnified throughout a congregation. And so, it was with great reluctance that I made up my mind not to compromise on what God had done for me, even if it meant leaving our denomination. Though he never said anything, I sensed my father's disappointment that I would not be following him. The rift between us widened.

It is ironic that years later, I learned that my mother's brother, Manley Pritchard, who pastored the largest Holiness church in Ottawa, had received the baptism in the Holy Spirit in the early days of this century, during the first modern outpouring of the Holy Spirit. He had kept silent about it, but I'm sure my mother must have known, and that explained why she had been so soft on the Pentecostals and had even taken me to some of their meetings. But at the time of the confrontation with my father, it looked like now he and I would never achieve the closeness I had so longed for.

When I graduated from grade thirteen, I decided to work for a year, to earn enough money to go to university. Two farmers up our way in Admaston and Cobden offered me summer jobs, and both were willing to pay $5.50 a day, plus room and board. Those were unheard of wages for a farmhand in those days, but they both knew I was a worker, and when Ross Faught also offered the use of his car on Friday nights to go dating, that swung the balance. I worked hard that summer, but in August, about the time I turned eighteen, I lined up a job at the magnesium mine—as a reduction helper in the research lab. The job paid $1.05 an hour, or about three dollars more per day than I could earn on the farm, and since the purpose of my working was to accumulate as much as I could as fast as possible for my education, Ross understood when I told him I would be leaving.

In the research lab, they were trying to improve on the plant's methods of reducing the amount of impurities in titanium and thorium. It was potentially dangerous work, because we were working with titanium powder in a heated vacuum. One of the things the other helper and I had to do was to remove a ten-inch, red-hot core sample from the laboratory's blast furnace and dispose of it in a waste barrel, making use of heavy-duty work gloves and tongs. I was doing this one evening, and did not know someone else had dumped titanium powder into the barrel ahead of me. When I dropped the core into the barrel, there was a tremendous explosion, and the next thing I knew I was picking myself up off the floor.

At first, I didn't realize what had happened. I looked down at my hands, and the cloth backs of the gloves I had been wearing were burned off. Then I began to feel pain in my face. The other helper had called the nurse, and I was rushed to the hospital in Renfrew. My eyebrows were gone, my scalp line was burned back, and the doctor said it was lucky I had apparently blinked my eyes shut at the moment the explosion occurred, or I would have been permanently blinded. But I took the whole thing pretty lightly, praising God for protecting me from any worse harm, and rather enjoying the attention of the hospital nurses for the next few days.

Eventually, I was well enough to go back to work, but I went back with a grievance: On the day shift, there were operators and a foreman responsible for the work in the lab, but on the evening shift, only two helpers were expected to carry the responsibility. I did not mind doing an operator's work, but I felt it was only fair that I be paid an equivalent wage of an additional twenty cents an hour, working with just one other helper on the evening shift.

So I decided to do something about it. I started a petition and got the signatures of some thirty workmen. And so that no one would have to put their name at the top of such a petition, I drew a circle on a large sheet of paper, and asked the men to sign around the circle. The wording of the petition was very meek, but a few days after it was submitted, I and the other evening-shift helper were laid off, without explanation.

That night, at the dinner table, as I related what had happened, I guess I expected some sympathy and support, especially as I had recently traded in my old Harley 74 for a '47 Plymouth four-door. That Plymouth was light blue and in remarkably good shape for 40,000 miles, and I still think it had the best lines of any cars I've seen. But I had had to take out a loan to get it, and I owed the finance company fifty-seven dollars a month—a hefty payment, when you are making only $1.05 an hour, and enormous when you are making nothing.

My father was furious. He had never financed anything in his life, he assured me, and he had never viewed the car as the necessity which I had seen it to be, in order to properly escort young ladies. And he continued in this vein for several minutes, reading me out in a manner that he hadn't done since back when we were at Annesley College. I, too, did something I hadn't done in years; I started to cry, and embarrassed, jumped up from the table and went to my room.

Throwing myself down on my bed, I buried my head in the patchwork quilt that was folded at the end of it, remembering this was the bed in which my mother had spent her last days at home. I bawled a great deal, feeling enormously sorry for myself. Here I was, deeply in debt, with no job and it was almost Christmas time, so no farmer needed help—and on and on went the litany of woe. I finally began to cry out to God.

Begging Him for guidance and direction, and repeating some of the many promises I had memorized in the Bible, a measure of peace came to me. I read His Word for the next couple of hours, battling returning bouts of self-pity.

Finally, when I knew God was in charge, I went back downstairs. "I was wrong to go into debt," I calmly told my father and Elva. "I am going to get a job, and I am going to make a go of it."

CHAPTER 7

Mr. Mainse

God *was* in charge, as it turned out. Once I had truly turned my situation over to Him, His solution was so unusual, and so much better than I could have possibly worked out that it was almost as if He was underlining the difference between His way of doing things and mine.

In those few days before Christmas, 1954, hearing of my plight, my sister Willa, who was teaching school in Pembroke about twenty-five miles up the highway from Haley's, called up the district school inspector. In those days, the school inspector was solely responsible for evaluating the performance of the pre-high school public schools and their staffs, and I could recall when Mr. Craig would come to our one-room schoolhouse. Our teacher would be under a good deal of stress, and if we liked him or her, which was usually the case, we would really work hard to make the best impression possible. Even so, Mr. Craig was a stern-visaged man and he almost never smiled.

Mr. Craig was still the school inspector when Willa called to tell him about her kid brother who had just graduated from grade thirteen with a good academic and athletic record, and who needed a job to earn money for university. Mr. Craig listened; he had rated Willa as one of the best teachers in his entire district, and her endorsement carried weight. None of this was known to me, however, when out of the blue, I received a call from him.

He told me of a four-room schoolhouse up in Chalk River, which was a small railroad town about twenty-five miles farther north, on the road to North Bay. One of the schoolrooms was empty, and the school board had decided to open it for the next semester. I could fill in as the interim teacher until the end of school, but if I wanted to continue in teaching, I would have to go to teachers' college, and earn my certificate. If I accepted, the pay would be $230 a month, and I would start immediately after the Christmas holidays. I accepted.

As it turned out, I was going to be put to more of a test than I had anticipated, for Mr. Craig had some additional information for me when I went into his office, just before leaving for Chalk River. Apparently, there had been a severe breakdown in discipline in that little school. Some of the boys in grades six, seven, and eight had failed those grades so many times that they were fifteen and sixteen years old. On two occasions, they had literally thrown the principal out the window of the school, and he had called the police.

"I am counting on you to be a settling influence, David," Mr. Craig concluded, without explaining exactly what he meant.

Driving up to Chalk River under an ominous, brooding sky, I noted that the road, which paralleled the Ontario-Quebec border, seemed to be reaching farther and farther into the wilderness. It was a wild, cold and raw country, and I shuddered and turned the heater up a notch. On either side of the road, tall jack pines loomed overhead, and I had the feeling that the wilderness itself was poised and brooding, and if man ever relinquished his grip, it would quickly reclaim all that had been carved out.

It was only four in the afternoon, but already shadows of dusk were gathering, and it would soon be dark. I checked the old Plymouth gas gauge and drove on, my mind now turning to classroom discipline and what I had observed over thirteen years as a student. Maintaining order—or the respect of the students, which was essentially the same thing—was a decidedly complex and individualistic thing. I had been in many situations where one group of kids would be perfectly behaved in one classroom, and the same group in another classroom, under a different teacher, would erupt into bedlam, and would remain unmanageable for the rest of the period. It did not seem to matter whether the teachers were men or women, young or old, large or small; if their classes were orderly, it was because they were respected. Some commanded respect, others earned it, and the best inspired it. But at eighteen years of age, I didn't know how to do any of the above.

And with that, the village of Chalk River appeared out of the gathering darkness. The village had a population of twelve hundred. Most of its inhabitants were involved with the roundhouse, which was one of the locomotive repair checkpoints on the Canadian Pacific's main line across the country. The rest of the men worked as laborers at the facilities of Atomic Energy of Canada. There were plenty of decent, churchgoing folks in Chalk River; there were also plenty of hard-drinking, two-fisted rounders. And their kids all went to the public school, or to the Catholic school.

Arrangements had been made for me to room with the Howards, a Roman Catholic family who became my good friends. Happily, I arrived just in time for supper. I went to bed early that night, and to school early the next morning. Two ladies taught the first four grades, and each had her own classroom. The principal himself taught grades seven and eight, which left me with grades five and six, where most of the problem students were.

From the steadily increasing noise level, it was obvious that the majority of students had arrived. The second semester would begin in a few minutes, and it was time to get my classroom ready for it.

As I reached for the door, I heard guffaws and muffled cheering; in my mind I turned the whole situation over to God and asked Him for at least the hundredth time to guide me by His Spirit. I opened the door and went in, and put my books and things on the desk. No one seemed to notice. Several older students in the fourteen-to-sixteen age bracket, mostly boys, were gathered at the back of the room, where two boys were arm wrestling. One of them, clearly their leader, was as big as I was. He had a fitting name (Herb Mussell) and his father was boss of all the yard crews over at the CP freight terminal.

Herb was in the fifth grade, had been for two years, and figured on remaining there for two more, until he turned seventeen and no longer legally had to attend school. In the meantime, he intended to have as much amusement in school as possible. This went for his cronies, as well, who had also failed repeatedly, though some had made it as far as the seventh and eighth grades. They were the honchos, and they called the shots with the younger kids, who were earning passing grades, either admiring them, or afraid to appear not to be. I smiled to myself; Mr. Craig had been typically conversative when he had spoken of a severe disciplinary breakdown. I walked up to the group and said, "Hello, I'm Mr. Mainse. I'll be taking the fifth and sixth grades this semester." There were a few hellos and phony smiles in my direction, and the attention quickly returned to the contest at hand. With a grin, Herb forced his opponent's arm down to the desk, and broadly acknowledged the acclaim from his classmates.

I knew what I had to do. Thank you, Lord, for helping me now, I thought, as I sat down across the desk from Herb. "Well," I said smiling, and putting my arm up on the desk, "let's have a go."

Herb looked at me, still grinning, then shrugged and put his big hand in mine, our forearms upright on the desk. Abruptly he nodded and applied sudden pressure, looking for a quick, decisive put-down. In that split second, I was grateful for every eighty-pound hay bale I had thrown, every tree I had felled, every time I had hit the blocking sled. I was able to hold him. Our arms remained locked in the upright position.

The grin was gone from Herb's face now, and the cheering from his supporters subsided and became more urgent. He began to strain, and still could not move me, and I realized then that I was going to win. But instead of quickly forcing his arm back, I let the battle go backwards and forwards a little, and then gradually put him down. I did that to allow him to save face among his friends, and only Herb knew what I was doing.

That was the first and last discipline crisis I had to face. There were problems, yes, but they were not crises. Herb and I became fast friends. Unbeknownst to him, I did a lot of praying for Herb, and the Lord soon showed me the reason he had fallen so far behind. It was not because he was stupid, but simply because he was full of mischief. In the ensuing weeks, he realized I really cared about his learning all he could, and he began to respond. He would come to me with his personal problems, and he also started applying himself to school work. I got him involved in what he was studying and then began to give him extra work, which he would do, and still more to do at night, until after a few weeks he was working to the maximum of his capacity—and asking for more. By the end of that semester, he had progressed to the point where he was doing seventh grade work.

Ronnie Culleton presented a different kind of problem. Short and wiry, red-headed and freckled, he might have weighed all of 120 pounds, with his overalls on. He was an intelligent fourteen-year-old student in the seventh grade, but he was even more full of mischief than Herb had been. He was the greatest discipline problem for the principal, for he had absolutely no respect for the man or his office—and I came to learn why. Ronnie had once seen the principal drunk in town.

It wasn't more than a day or two before the principal noticed the classroom next to his was actually quiet, and before long he decided to make me his enforcer of discipline. I would be in the middle of a teaching session when there would be a rap on the door, and it would be the principal. "Mr. Mainse, would you come and discipline Ronald?" He was my superior, and I had no choice, so I would invite Ronnie into the hall and have a quiet talk with him. The first couple of times, this sufficed. But I sensed that Ronnie was wondering how far I could be pushed, and that eventually he would have to find out. For the moment, however, he was not quite ready for a showdown.

And then one day, he decided the time had come. He was in my classroom with some of my students, and as I approached the door, he locked me out. My first impulse was to break the door down, but instead I prayed a speedy prayer. It came to me in a flash, and I ran outside the building. Between the outer door to the classroom and the room itself was a cloakroom with a window in it, which we usually left cracked for fresh air. The sill was eight feet from the ground. I jumped up, grabbed the sill with one hand, pushed the window up with the other, and hoisted myself up and in through the window. I came barreling out of that cloakroom like a Mack truck and grabbed Ronnie, his eyes wide as saucers, by the scruff of the neck. I gave him a very sound strapping for that, and that was the last time he crossed me.

It was not, however, the last time he created a disturbance. One afternoon there was a rap on the door, and I was once more summoned next-door to deal with Ronnie. When I went into the principal's classroom, I had to bite my lip to keep from smiling. Ronnie had moved his desk against the back wall and was perched there defiantly. A huge St. Bernard was sitting next to him. As if to demonstrate to me what had been going on, the principal said, "Now, Ronald, do this work!"

"Make me," Ronnie replied, grinning back at him.

The principal walked toward the back of the room and approached Ronald. The St. Bernard drew back its jowls and showed its teeth, letting out a deep, menacing growl, and drooling all over the place. Apparently this little drama had repeated itself numerous times before the principal came to get me. He turned to me, hands on hips, to see what I would do.

I knew this dog. I had made it a point to call on the families of each child in my classes, and Ronnie's younger brother, Gene, was in grade six. When I visited the Culletons', I had gotten to know their dog, too, so now I went up to him, like an old friend, and patted him, and he wagged his tail affectionately.

I considered using the strap again on Ronnie, but realized he was the sort of person who would regard it as a status symbol, and so I simply said, "Okay, Ronnie, you've had your fun. Now take the dog outside, and tie him up or send him home." He did as he was told, and I hoped that would end the problem.

But the principal couldn't forget it, and the next time Ronnie acted up, they got into a shouting match, and this time, instead of calling me, the principal called the police. I never did find out what it was all about, but I now became concerned for Ronnie's future, because the principal did have the authority to expel Ronnie, once and for all, and was saying he intended to do so. I offered to take Ronnie into my room, and the offer was accepted.

I did not know what it was about Chalk River, but suddenly I found my heart was overflowing in concern for these people. For instance, there was a Jewish girl in grade five, named Sandra Levine, whose family had a general store. When I visited her family, I learned that her father liked to play chess but had no one to play with, so I had him teach me how, and would play with him during quiet afternoons in the store—occasionally taking the opportunity to share a little about the Messiah with him.

It finally began to warm up in the spring. I got the boys outside to play baseball. Finding that there was no league, I went to Deep River to see Fr. Harrington, pastor of the Catholic church who was responsible for the separate school there, and then saw the principal of the public school and the head of the Chalk River separate school. Together we formed our own league. Because of the number of older boys in our grades who came to school two hours early every morning to practice, Chalk River never lost a game, but all the schools were happy to be involved in a league.

The most exciting thing that happened in that spring of '55 was the Sunday school. I discovered that a lot of the children in our school were not going to Sunday school anywhere, and when I encouraged them to go to one of the existing Sunday schools in town, they were simply not interested. Nor were their parents. There were five churches in Chalk River, more than enough to take care of everyone, but I found that the memberships were inclined to be clannish. These church members gained much of their personal identities through their church affiliation, and consequently those in town who did not already go to church were not about to start.

So I started a Sunday school. Pastor Bombay from Pembroke helped me rent the old Orange Hall for Sunday afternoons, and before long, we had twenty-five kids coming. Joyce Bombay and other Pembroke young people drove up every Sunday to help. And then, some of the parents of our children asked if we wouldn't have a service for them, too. And since almost all of them were people who didn't have a church, we did not feel that to do so would be "sheep stealing," so we started having afternoon services.

At first there weren't more than six or eight adults who came, but it was as if there were a hundred times that number as I preached my heart out to them. Joyce taught Sunday school with equal fervor. And I became involved in the lives of those Chalk River people. I had already met quite a number of them from my calls on the families of the children in my class, which calls I now extended to the families of all the children in our school.

After a while, they came to think of me in pastoral terms. They knew I wasn't ordained, but they also knew I was going to Bible college in the fall, and would be a minister one day, so in their minds, it was almost the same thing. I used to go fishing with old Win Johnson, a retired railroad engineer, whose stories of train crashes and near misses kept me enthralled by the hour. I was a good listener, and when it came his turn to listen, he was too, and I was able to lead him to the Lord. When he died a few weeks later of a heart attack, his widow, May, insisted that I take the service. I begged off, because I wasn't ordained, but she would have no one else, and so I had a long talk with the United Church minister about it. He said I should make May Johnson happy, and he loaned me his funeral book.

Another time, I had gone to bed when one of the boys in the eighth grade, who had a younger brother in my class, burst into the Howards' in a panic. "Mr. Mainse! You gotta come quick! My dad's drunk, and he's got a knife—"

I got dressed as fast as I could, and ran after him. The scene in his house was horrifying. His four younger sisters and brothers, the youngest barely three, were cowering together in a corner. The father was in a rage, brandishing a large butcher knife with which he had already slashed his wife deeply in the breast. She was bleeding terribly and screaming.

"Oh, Jesus!" I exclaimed aloud, "if you've ever helped me, help me now!" And with that, the father turned on me.

"In the name of Jesus," I shouted at him, surprised at the authority in my voice, *"put that knife down!"* He stopped and looked at me.

"You heard me," I said, "I've come here in the name of Jesus, and I tell you to PUT THAT KNIFE DOWN!" And he did. The moment he did, all the fight seemed to go out of him. I said to him: "You've cut your wife, and I've got to take her to the hospital, and you've terrified your children, *now you sit down!"* He did, and I knew he would be no more trouble. Getting the wife to press a towel against herself as tight as she could to stop the bleeding, I ran to get my car and was back in a minute. "C'mon kids, get in," I called, "we're all going with your mom to the hospital." I couldn't leave them alone in the house with him. It took sixteen stitches to close up the wound, and as the doctor was working on her, I started to tremble.

Only then did I realize how scared I had been.

When school finally let out, our fledgling church was growing so that I knew I couldn't leave Chalk River. I had grown to love the town and the people, and many of them apparently reciprocated, for they asked Mr. Craig, the school inspector, if, since he had already made one exception in my case, he wouldn't make another. Apparently he, too, was pleased with all that had taken place. I was told that if I would go to summer school that summer, I could take over as principal of the school in the fall.

I was deeply touched; I was only eighteen and knew what an exception was being made. They wanted me to be their principal indefinitely, and told me that if I would go to summer school for five years, that would be the equivalent of teachers' college, and I would then be eligible for the necessary teaching certificate.

But as much as I loved teaching from the little taste I'd had of it, I loved pastoring even more. I wanted to teach about Jesus, not Latin or geometry or social studies. I couldn't put aside the clear and distinct call to go into the ministry. And so I thanked them and told them my decision.

That summer, I was able to get a job as a carpenter's helper at the atomic energy plant, which enabled me to earn additional money for Bible college, enabling me to stay in the Chalk River area. With Joyce Bombay's help, I organized a two-week daily vacation Bible school and got permission to use the school building. I was even able to bring in Mary Scobie, who had been my own daily vacation Bible school teacher when I was a boy in my father's church. In August, we had an old-time tent revival, and by the time I went down to Eastern Pentecostal Bible College in Peterborough that September, our church had twenty-five to thirty in regular attendance. I felt it was strong enough as a body to stand together, and I had lined up a young minister who was willing to come to be their shepherd.

Bible college was everything had I hoped it would be—exciting, challenging, and filled with other young people who were as much on fire for the Lord as I was. I studied harder than I ever had in my life, and wound up third in my class of sixty. The fellowship was exciting, too; there were young men in our class like Albert Vaters and Paul Tinlin. Paul, a second-year student, Ron Stevens, and I formed a trumpet trio and traveled around, playing in area churches.

Only one thing dampened my unremitting joy. I had hoped my father might be pleased with my going to Bible college, but the fact that it was a Pentecostal college made all the difference to him. When I enrolled, he gave me a thousand dollars, but so that I wouldn't mistake that for approval, he told me he had given each of my sisters the same amount when they had gotten married. "It looks like you're going to need it now, rather than later," was all he said.

One other thing depressed me: the young minister who was supposed to be shepherding the little flock in Chalk River got an invitation to take the pulpit of an established church, and left abruptly. I couldn't judge him too harshly; it was a very small congregation to begin with, and I had not felt they were at a place where they could understand the principle of tithing.

Joyce Bombay was still making the weekly trek up there to teach Sunday school, but services had stopped. And even though she wrote encouraging letters to me, the fate of the little church weighed on me heavily.

In February, I developed an acute sinus infection which raised my temperature to 106 degrees. I had been born in a little village parsonage, and my sinuses had not been checked to make sure that they were open. The left sinus was closed, and as a result it had become inflamed many times over the years. There were periods in Ottawa when I practically lived on painkillers. The repeated inflammations had eaten away the bone between the sinus cavity and the brain. Now, the doctors were afraid that the current infection would enter the brain.

They dared not move me from my bed at the Bible college, and one doctor, a specialist, told Rev. Found, the president of the college, and Dr. Ratz, the dean of theology, that the only way I would leave the college would be feet first. But those two gentlemen had a different view. After the doctors left, they came in, and though I was swimming in a delirium, I remember them laying hands on my head. And then they prayed in the name of Jesus for my healing.

It felt like a cooling shower had just come on my head and flowed down over my entire body, and with it, the fever was washed away. Simultaneously, the terrible pressure behind and above my left eye released. The pus that was there broke down into the eye socket. It was a revolting mess; my eyeball was lying almost on my cheek, with all that infection behind it. But it had not entered my brain. I went into the hospital, and in a few days I was out again and back in action.

That spring of 1956, as soon as the roads were passable, our trumpet trio headed north for a long weekend of playing and holding services up in mining country—Haleyburg on Friday night, Timmins on Saturday night, Matheson Sunday morning, and Kirkland Lake Sunday night. On that last night, God laid a message on my heart unlike any I had ever given before—I was to preach on hell. Up to that night, I usually worked out what I was going to say pretty carefully, with a good deal of preparation, just as I would for the classroom.

But this night was different. When I rose to preach, I ignored my scribbled notes. An anointing came over me that was so strong I felt like I was down in the front row, listening to someone else preach. It amounted to a prophetic utterance, expressing some of the immense compassion of Christ for the lost. When I finished, six people came forward to accept Christ as Lord and Saviour.

Unbeknownst to me, the pastor of the church, Clayton Warriner, had been taping my message, and he gave me a copy of it. It was on a quarter-inch reel (cassettes had not yet been invented in those days), and I wondered what to do with it. I asked the Lord, and the thought came to send it to my father, who had never heard me preach.

A couple of weeks later, a letter from my father arrived at Bible college. In addition to bits of family news, there was this encouraging word: "Thank you for the tape. I shared it with my evening prayer meetings at Haley's and Admaston. Since you are going to be home for Easter, perhaps you would consider preaching for me on Easter Sunday."

I wept.

CHAPTER 8

"I Love You, Norma-Jean"

What a thrill it was to preach my first Easter sermon in my father's church! Tears sprang to my eyes when at one point I happened to glance in my father's direction and see tears in his eyes. He didn't say anything afterwards; he didn't have to. God had done a deep work in both of us, and during the rest of that Easter holiday, I knew we were close for the first time.

I took this gift of a new relationship with my father as a definite encouragement from the Lord, and I could hardly wait for the spring semester to be over, so I could get back up to Chalk River to work with the people I loved. And now I received a second, even stronger, encouragement: the Pembroke Church, which had periodically provided such helpers as Joyce Bombay, learning of my intent to reopen the Orange Hall, had also learned that I needed to earn money for my second year in Bible college. They offered to pay my tuition at Bible college the next year, if I would reopen the work at Chalk River that summer and devote my full time and energy to it. Dancing for joy, I immediately got out a sketch pad and pencil and started designing the poster to announce the formal reopening of the church in the Orange Hall. This time, there would be no more afternoon services; we were going to have church at eleven in the morning and an evening service at seven, just like the established churches! Only Sunday school would remain in the afternoon.

Only a few of the regulars from the summer before showed up that first Sunday; there might have been a dozen people in all. But I was not discouraged; God was with us, and I had experienced small beginnings before. In our Sunday school, I was glad to see Johnny and Randy Schultz back, and they brought their little sister. She hadn't started school yet, but she could sing at the top of her voice, and usually did. Her favorite hymn, which she requested every Sunday, was the "Popsicle Hymn"—"Only believe, only believe, all things are *popsicle*—" The way she sang it gave it a sense all its own.

Now that I didn't have another job to take my time, I helped to organize a meeting across the Ottawa River in Quebec, in a heavy machinery garage. Also, making use of the little family cottage which my father and I had built by a lake not far from his birthplace, I organized a week-long Bible camp for six of the boys in our church. We discovered that there was something very special about getting together and having good Christian fellowship in an outdoors setting, and it was an experience I would file away for the future.

By the time I was due to return to Bible college for the second year, our congregation had grown to more than thirty people—still not enough to make me sure of its standing through the coming winter. And so, after much prayer, I made a hard decision: I would put off returning to Bible college for a year, or until such time as the church was ready to stand on its own, with or without a pastor.

But I had so many friends in Bible college by now that I couldn't bear the thought of not seeing them all for a year, so I went down for the welcoming party for the new class. It was great seeing everyone again—Albert and Paul and Ron, and of course Wally, my first-year roommate. It was a wonderful party, and a nice-looking young couple sang a duet: "I woke up this morning with heaven on my mind."

"Who are they?" I casually asked Wally.

"Ralph Rutledge, who's a first-year student, and his sister, Norma-Jean."

"His sister, you say?" and I eyed the young lady with the large brown eyes and shoulder-length dark hair with renewed interest.

"Relax," Wally chuckled, "she's only sixteen." And with a shrug, I shifted my concentration elsewhere.

All too soon, it was time for me to head back to Chalk River, and it was tearing me apart to have to leave. As we said goodbye, I told Wally, only half kidding, to leave his window cracked at night. Because if I ever got cabin fever up there, I intended to drive the hundred and eighty miles even if it was late at night, and the college locked its gates at eleven. Little did I realize that before the year was out, I would be availing myself of Wally's hospitality for some desperately needed fellowship.

There was a lovely Indian summer in the Ottawa Valley that October—warm, balmy days, with the leaves of the occasional maples flaming red. I enjoyed tramping in the woods on Sunday afternoons, much as I had years before on the farm at Ramsayville. But the days were growing shorter, and the nights colder, and an ominous quietude began to settle over Chalk River, presaging a long winter.

More brooding thunderclouds gathered on my horizon. I woke up one morning in early October, and for the forty-third day, made myself a lonely breakfast. Setting the little table for one, I poured out the customary bowl of cornflakes and reached in the refrigerator for some milk. There wasn't any: I had forgotten that I had finished it off the morning before. I sat down in silence, said the blessing, and stared morosely at the dry cornflakes. Then I slowly put a dry spoonful in my mouth and chewed and swallowed and put another spoonful in and chewed and swallowed—and a great big tear rolled down my cheek and plopped into the cornflakes.

I got up from the table and went over and knelt by my bed and gave in to a first-class pity party. I could have charged some milk and other groceries at Mr. Levine's store, for though I had not succeeded in having him receive his Messiah, he was fond of me and would have given me credit. But I had learned a lot about indebtedness from my own mistakes and others' and one of the things I had learned was that you don't ever start borrowing for regularly recurring expenses, like groceries, because that kind of debt runs away from you in no time.

But what was I going to do, I wondered. At the most the collection each Sunday was around three or four dollars, which would simply not support a person, and I was less inclined than ever to bring up the principle of tithing, because I had come to know just how little most of these people had. "Oh, God!" I cried out, "I have never asked you for money before; I've always been able to earn whatever I needed. But now I've got nowhere else to turn."

I went on praying, and in the course of my prayers, I confessed my self-pity, and my unbelief, and my pride, and everything else I could think of, and gradually an assurance came over me that He really *was* in charge. Then I got a nudge to go to the post office. An envelope was waiting there for me—no name, no return address. It contained a five-dollar bill. I let out such a whoop that one lady scowled disapprovingly at me, and I never did find out who sent that money.

That was only the beginning of God's provision. The following month, the new principal of the public school, a lady this time, needed to go into the hospital for an operation, and the school board asked me if I would take over as principal for the month of November. I praised God for an hour after that offer: the money I would earn in that month would keep me in cornflakes and milk for the rest of the winter! And on top of that, in December I did odd-job work as a carpenter around Camp Petawawa, the nearby army camp, and earned enough money for Christmas presents.

But by December, the loneliness was really getting to me. One evening the fog was so thick it looked like a white blanket outside my window, and I finally reached the point where I couldn't stand it another minute. I grabbed my parka and headed out the door; I was going down to Peterborough, as fast as I could go, and having made the decision, I felt better already. But as fast as I could go was not going to be very fast. The fog was so thick I could barely find the car. My Plymouth was ten years old now, and rusted badly enough that there was a gaping hole in the floorboards, to the left of the clutch. That hole came in handy that night. Once I got on the highway, I took the flashlight I kept in the glove compartment and shined it down through the hole, to pick up the white line in the center of the road. That way, I was able to make some headway, and finally reached the Bible college some time after three.

During previous visits, I had met a girl who was a student at the college. She had a lovely face, figure and personality. I saw her again on this trip and I thought about her a lot on the long drive back, and indeed I thought about little else for the next few days. Finally, I did something very rash: I called her up and proposed to her. Startled, she said she would have to think about it, and would get back to me. And now I began to have some qualms—could it be that I had acted in any way out of self-pity at the prospect of that long, long winter ahead? "Well, Lord," I said somewhat belatedly, "if I have acted out of foolishness, or impure motives, I pray you will give her more good sense than I have. If this is not in your plan for me at this time, then please put a stop to it now." He did. She called back two days later to turn me down.

After Christmas, winter did indeed come to Chalk River. At times there was so much snow that the province's plows did not even attempt to cope with it, except on the main highway, and not even there on weekends. One night, I was out with my car, trying to tow another man's car to the gas station, to help him get it started, and the thermometer by the station's front door registered fifty degrees below zero!

On some particularly cold and windy Sunday mornings, the oil stove in the Orange Hall was unable to push the mercury more than a few degrees above freezing. On those mornings, we would keep our coats on and get as close to the stove as we could. And then we would sing many hymns. My mother, who had a degree from the Ontario Conservatory of Music and was a licensed teacher with the Royal Conservatory, had started me on the piano, but when my father came home from Egypt, he did not consider piano-playing worth exercising the discipline to keep his son at it, so I had dropped it. But that summer and fall in Chalk River, I had picked it up again and learned all the hymns. I could only play one or two at a time on those freezing mornings, before the cold would cause my fingers to stiffen up, and I'd have to put my hands in my pockets.

One Sunday evening, with a howling blizzard going on outside, only one man showed up for the service. I debated what to do and decided that if he had made that much of an effort to come, we would have a service, even if it was just the two of us. That night, in between prayers and Scripture readings and a brief sermon, I announced hymns which we sang together, I played the piano, and played the guitar and even played the trumpet, and then gave an altar call. And when Whitney came forward to pray at the altar, the Lord reached down and baptized him in the Holy Spirit. That night was one of the happiest in his life—and mine.

That was the sort of glorious strengthening the Lord was giving us in the midst of our trials. Further encouragement came soon after: the Pentecostal district superintendent, anxious for me to return to Bible college and become ordained, said the district would now stand behind the work and send someone in the fall, when I was due to go back to college, to stay and see that the work was carried on.

In the late spring, when it finally began to warm up, my spirits began to lift. As a way to get to know the people of Chalk River, I joined the local baseball team, and got to play second base. It was a hardball league, a small one—Deep River (six miles away), Petawawa, Pembroke and Beechburg. I didn't score any home runs, but I managed to put them between the infield and the outfield often enough to wind up the season with a .390 average.

That summer, our attendance on Sundays rose to a high of forty-two, and I had hopes that it would continue to grow. The district sent a young fellow just out of Bible college to take over in the fall, and they subsidized him and his wife with home missions funds. I gave them my dear old Plymouth as a gift, and went back to college.

My former classmates were a year ahead of me, but that had no effect on our fellowship. And in my class now was Ralph Rutledge, the fellow with the brown-eyed sister. Ralph and I hit it off from the start, and he and my roommate, Maurice Fostry, and I soon laid plans to form a group, to travel around preaching and playing on weekends.

There was just one trouble with Ralph; his kid sister was coming up to the college for a weekend visit, and he wanted one of us to take her out. I really wasn't interested, because she was so young, and neither was Maurice, but finally I said, "Oh, well, I'll do it." And I resigned myself to a dutiful weekend, which I determined to endure cheerfully, because I liked Ralph and was glad to do him the favor.

When his sister arrived on the Saturday afternoon train, I was again struck by her beauty—what a pity she was only, let's see, seventeen by now. And she had a quick-spirited, light and lively personality to go with her looks—but I was twenty-one, and not about to "rob the cradle." That evening, we went over to Aunt Ethel's; she was *the* lady of fashion in Peterborough, having married the cousin of a British earl. She also had the only color television set we knew of in town, with a huge antenna to pull in the signal across Lake Ontario, from Rochester, where the nearest color broadcasting was being done.

During the course of the evening, it came out that Norma-Jean was not seventeen but going on nineteen—and suddenly our blind date took on a whole new dimension. In the car on the way back, just as we were pulling into the college yard, I reached over and held her hand. She not only let me do this, but just before we got out of the car, she gave my hand a little squeeze. That may seem old-fashioned today, but in those days a look or a touch counted, and my heart did an aerial maneuver or two before settling back in my chest.

I went down to the train station with Ralph to see Norma-Jean off, but I am not sure with how much fervor I would have pursued her, had it not been for her brother. As soon as we got in the car and headed back to college, he started in. "David, you should write to her."

"Well, I do like her—"

"Then you'd better tell her, because she's got a lot of other guys interested in her."

Even so, I put off writing for a week, and when I did, all I said was that I had enjoyed the evening, and that I hoped I would see her again sometime. Not too romantic, and neither was her reply. But there is some truth to that old saw about absence making the heart grow fonder. I wasn't particularly interested in any of the girls in college or around town, and I found myself thinking more and more about her, wondering what she thought about certain things, like how she would react to things that happened in the classes I was in, and so on. In my letters I began to share a little of what I was thinking, and our correspondence began to pick up momentum.

It got a supernatural boost from something which happened up in Perth, where our group was ministering on a Sunday evening. I had had a tremendous burden all that day to pray for Norma-Jean to receive the baptism in the Holy Spirit. If she was the one God had picked for me—and as I've indicated, long, drawn-out beginnings were not my style—then she would need the same infilling of the Holy Spirit in the Book of Acts way that I had received. So, after the service, I went down to the prayer room in the basement and started to pray for her to receive the baptism. But I could not pray at all. It could mean only one thing: there was no more need to pray.

I ran to find Ralph and tell him that his sister had just received the baptism, even though she was home in Galt, two hundred miles away! So we just praised the Lord, and two days later two letters arrived for Ralph, confirming that on Sunday night, during their usual evening service, Norma-Jean had been praying and suddenly received such an infilling of the Spirit that she was inebriated with joy. And at the same time, she had been healed of an abscess at the base of her spine which had been plaguing her for two years, and which was the reason she thought she had gone forward for prayer.

By the time I saw her again, my heart had done quite a job on me. It was two weeks later, the last weekend in November, and our group was playing near her hometown of Galt. Norma-Jean came to hear us, and afterwards, I took her for a moonlight walk in the park. We paused under a lonely streetlight, and I asked if I might kiss her. She nodded gravely, but there was a twinkle in her big brown eyes as she tilted her head up to me.

That kiss sealed it; I was in love! The "Dear Norma-Jean/Dear David" express went highballing down the main line after that. I wrote her as often as I could, and she wrote frequently. I went home for Christmas, and had a good time with my family—the best since mom had died, in fact. Dad had been elected General Superintendent of Eastern Canada and, while he didn't think for health reasons he could assume the responsibility, he was tremendously pleased to be asked. He and others had worked long, hard and diplomatically to bring about the impending union between the Holiness Movement churches and the Free Methodists, and now this honor was the crowning moment of his illustrious career.

My own holidays hit their high point after I got back to college, and was invited to come down to the Rutledge home for New Year's Eve and New Year's Day. On New Year's Eve, we went over to Buffalo, New York, to a black church there, for a watch night service. The whole Rutledge family was musical (Norma-Jean's father owned a music store, and in addition to all of them singing, her brother Glen was an expert trombonist and brothers, Reynold and Harold, were superb on the marimba). The church we were going to, the Church of God in Christ, was reputed to have the best music in North America. That may not have been an exaggeration.

After midnight, as the service was winding down a bit, Norma-Jean and I slipped out to the car. We talked a little, and then I couldn't wait any longer: "How would you like to marry a fellow like me—not a fellow like me, but *me*?"

She just smiled and said, "Yes, I do want to marry you."

The next day the Rutledge family had a turkey dinner with all the fixings—stuffing, potatoes, gravy, creamed onions, squash, salad, cranberry sauce and pecan pie. And because Norma-Jean's mother had been killed by a drunken driver the previous spring, Norma-Jean had done all the cooking herself. I was amazed, and marveled at God's wisdom! (In later years, as I've occasionally had trouble buttoning a vest, I've wished she weren't such a good cook—but only until the next meal.)

I was busy at college the next couple of months, so several weeks would go by before we would be able to see each other. But rain, snow, and sleet were not preventing the postmen from making their appointed rounds, as absence now made two hearts grow fonder.

Actually, a good deal of what little spare time I had that winter was spent playing basketball. There is a common impression that if a Bible college has a basketball team, it's unusual, and is bound to be a pushover. I guess we surprised a few people—on the courts, as well as in the bleachers. We beat every team in our area, most of them twice.

The remaining extracurricular time was spent with our traveling music group. I was particularly grateful for the trips, because every so often, we would be within visiting distance of Norma-Jean. One Saturday afternoon in late March, we were in Toronto to play at the Danforth Gospel Temple the next morning. Norma-Jean was staying with friends in town, and we went for a walk in a lakefront park. It was a beautiful spring afternoon, with the sun beginning to feel warm for the first time.

We sat down on a bench, looking out on the calm surface of the lake, where the afternoon sun broke into shimmering crescents on the water. I pointed to a man who was walking along the path approaching us, and as Norma-Jean turned to look at him, I took her left hand and slipped an engagement ring on the third finger. Her large brown eyes grew larger, and she was speechless. I was delighted, having picked it out myself and gotten a special deal from Maurice Fostry's uncle who was a jeweler. Even so, it had depleted my savings—but it was more than worth it.

Not long after that, I took her to meet my father and Elva. They lived in Kingston now, where dad was pastoring a Free Methodist church; the merger with the Free Methodists had been successful, and the Holiness Movement churches no longer existed. Dad was obviously pleased with Norma-Jean at first sight. He agreed to perform the wedding service along with Rev. Fredrickson, the pastor of Norma-Jean's church in Galt, where the wedding would take place on September 19.

In the meantime, things got busier than ever at college. I was elected president of the student council, and our touring ensemble had grown to include a bass fiddle, a guitar, an accordion and a piano, along with the original three trumpets. It broke up at the end of the college year, with most of the guys having other plans for the summer, but Ralph, Maurice and I, three members of the original group, decided we would keep on touring the whole summer. We bought a second-hand Ford wagon to carry our instruments and equipment, and we set a policy which made a remarkable difference in our delivery, and our ability to hear the Lord as we played or preached. For every minute we expected to spend performing, we would spend a minute in prayer together beforehand. (To this day, before each hour-and-a-half live TV broadcast, I will spend an hour and a half in prayer.) And we did the same thing before our practice sessions, spending as much time praying as we did practicing. All over Ontario, people who had heard many gospel singers and musicians commented that there was something different about this group. I believe the difference was the amount of time we spent in prayer together.

The nineteenth of September, 1958, a date that I had waited for more impatiently than any other in my life, finally arrived. Wallace Johnson was my best man, and when my vision of loveliness in white came down the aisle, I could hardly believe it was actually happening. It was like a wide-awake dream come true. The minister's voice even had a dream-like quality, as he read the treasured words: "Wilt thou, David, take Norma-Jean to be thy lawful, wedded wife, to live together after God's ordinance in the holy estate of matrimony? Wilt thou love her, comfort her, honour, and keep her in sickness and in health; and, forsaking all others, keep thee only unto her, so long as ye both shall live?"

Beautiful. With a start, I realized that people were waiting for me to respond. "I will!" I exclaimed, and everyone laughed.

CHAPTER 9

The Hidden Support

We had been back in the Bible college's married quarters just three days, and had hardly gotten into the routine of the school year, when I got a call from Keith Running. A fairly recent graduate of the college himself, Keith had pioneered a church in the little community of Brighton, about ninety miles east of Toronto, on the north shore of Lake Ontario. "David, can you come down this Wednesday evening and preach for a call? I've received one myself to another church, and we feel you're the person the Lord has picked to take my place."

"But, Keith, I'm still in my third year of Bible college—"

"We know that, but you could drive back and forth on the weekends, and we would be able to pay you twenty dollars a week."

"No, I really don't think—"

"David, just come down for this one Wednesday and keep your heart open; that's all. You wouldn't want to miss the Lord, would you?" he said laughing, and reluctantly I agreed to go.

Norma-Jean begged off, pleading a headache, though I suspected she was a bit overwhelmed at the imminent prospect of becoming a pastor's wife at age nineteen. So off I went and gave it my best shot. There was a surprising number of young people in the congregation. I liked their spirit, and it was easy to preach to them. After the service was over, the deacons did offer me a call, and I had an increasingly good feeling about it. And so I became the pastor of Evangel Temple, the newest, smallest, and possibly liveliest church in Brighton.

Every Friday after classes, Norma-Jean and I would drive down from Peterborough and stay in the little parsonage that had been built on the end of the church. Our car was a six-year-old Pontiac, given to us as a wedding present by Norma-Jean's father, and no matter how cold the weather, the car never failed us. Our membership was only thirty or forty, with fifty-five or sixty children in Sunday school, but the presence of God's Holy Spirit was so powerful that everyone was aware of Him. Every weekend, people were getting saved and filled with the Spirit and physically healed; in effect, what we were experiencing was nothing less than revival!

"O Lord!" I rejoiced one evening, "if this is what the ministry is going to be like from here on in, it will be fantastic!" And then, when I got back to campus that Sunday evening, He showed me that it had nothing to do with me whatever, or my ability to preach or pastor, other than my obedience in speaking and doing what the Spirit gave me. That night, I slipped into the men's prayer room, which was separated from the women's prayer room by a partition. As I was about to pray, I heard someone on the women's side mention my name. Someone was praying for David Mainse, that God would bless and anoint his ministry, and through it would perform miracles of healing.

It had a profound effect on me, and I knelt there a long time, just letting the Lord teach me about intercessory prayer. The first thing He showed me was that, since I was the only member of the student body going out regularly in a ministerial capacity, all the students were regularly praying for my ministry and my church. That undergirding of prayer was the main reason that so many exciting things happened in Brighton.

God showed me how much He valued my mother's prayers for me, all those early years when I had been too much for her to handle, and her later prayers for my future life. And my father's prayers too, for there was nothing he could do but pray when he was over in Egypt, and I was in such rebellion at boarding school. Were it not for the prayers of my father and mother—and the surrendered lives they lived which gave their prayers such power—there is no telling what would have become of me. When prayer is there, grace abounds. When it isn't there, the identical work or ministry can be reduced to a tenth, or a hundredth, of its effectiveness, as I was to discover.

When we went back down to Brighton the following weekend, it was with a sober sense that we were merely instruments, that whatever happened, it was a sovereign act of God, in response to prayer and obedience and His master plan, and that it had nothing to do with us.

That Sunday, one of our regulars, an older diabetic lady named Mrs. Fritz, had to be led into church. She had had a reaction to an overdose of insulin, and it had blinded her. When the hospital discharged her, telling her that there was nothing medically that they could do for her, she asked some friends to bring her to church. They had to lead her in; she had only a tiny bit of sight left in one eye, and no vision at all in the other.

When I was informed of what had happened, I asked her friends to bring her forward, saying, "Jesus is the same, yesterday, today and forever." And laying my hands over her eyes, I said firmly, "Eyes, be opened in the name of Jesus!" Then I held up my Bible in front of her, and holding my hand over the eye which still had some sight, I said, "Now, Mrs. Fritz, read!"

She shook her head. "I do see something—but it's all blurry."

"That's all right; that happened with Jesus once too. A blind man whom He healed at first saw men 'only as trees walking.' So Jesus prayed again." I prayed also, and this time, when I removed my hand from her blind eye, Mrs. Fritz could read the Bible clearly. It happened to be open to the twenty-third Psalm, and she read through it without a mistake. By the time she got to, "Yea, though I walk through the valley of the shadow of death, I will fear no evil, for thou art with me—" you could no longer hear her voice over the tumultuous praises and hallelujahs. Our eyes had seen His glory, and He was truly marching on!

It was hard to keep my mind on my studies after that, but I had only half a year left before I graduated, and I did my best to bear down.

Graduation came on a warm night in June, and took place in Toronto, in beautiful Massey Hall. Our class was called the "Witnesses," and across the back of the stage hung a huge banner that said, "Witnesses, you are my witnesses." The number of men and women who went on into evangelism or the mission field or to pastoring is remarkable. God saw fit to pour out His Spirit that night, and the ceremony and speeches and singing were everything each of us had hoped they would be.

And so, in the summer of 1959, Norma-Jean and I bade farewell to Peterborough and moved down to the little village of Brighton. One of the first things we did was to ask permission from the town council to hold outdoor street meetings on Saturday nights, on Main Street, and a bylaw was duly enacted, granting us that permission for each Saturday at 7:00 P.M. Every week you would find Norma-Jean and me and a growing number of our young people out there among the farmers who were filling the streets as they did their shopping. I played the trumpet and Norma-Jean played the accordion, only now she had to do so as far out in front of her as she could reach, as she was expecting our first child.

I had suggested that she might want to take it easy on Saturday nights, but she wouldn't hear of it. She never did miss a Saturday night, not even when Elaine was born at the end of June. And frankly, I was just as glad, because in the beginning, those street meetings were hard. At first, I could not figure out what the matter was; everything and everyone, ourselves included, seemed somewhat lethargic. And it was not simply because we were in the center of town; our church meetings were that way too. And then it struck me. Of course! With college out, no one was in the prayer rooms, praying for us! So, the next Sunday was devoted to teaching and testimonies and sharing on the subject of intercessory prayer. As a result, those present agreed to take on the church and its outreach as a personal prayer concern. We all determined to establish our own prayer life, and we put up a prayer-concern bulletin board, and set up a prayer chain. Everyone, whether they could help on Saturday nights or not, agreed to pray for the street meetings, as they went about whatever they were doing.

The difference was immediate and dramatic! And one of the most extraordinary coincidences occurred as a direct result of that prayer support. It happened on the first Saturday in July, which was the Saturday after Elaine was born. The Queen was visiting Canada that summer, and the first night of her arrival, she was scheduled to be the guest of the governor general, Vincent Massey, at his home in Port Hope. The Queen's plane was due to land at Trenton Air Force Base, eight miles to the east of us, and she would travel by motorcade to Port Hope, twenty-seven miles to the west of us. There was only one route that linked the two locations, Highway 2, and it ran right through the middle of Brighton. What was more, the Queen's flight was due to land around six o'clock Saturday evening.

Five thousand people joined the citizens of Brighton to jam both sides of Main Street for its full length. At five minutes to seven, everyone was craning to see as far as they could down to the east end of town, and Norma-Jean, sparky as ever, with tiny Elaine well-wrapped and tucked in her carriage, was there by my side. Our helpers were close about us when the cry first went up, "Here they come!"

I couldn't see anything at first, except the backs of the heads of others who were looking at the heads of those next to them and so on. Finally, up the street in the distance came three Mounties on motorcycles wearing scarlet tunics. I glanced at my watch: two minutes to seven, and I felt again in my breast pocket, to make sure I had the town's permit to hold an assembly at seven.

As the gleaming, open Cadillac carrying the Queen came into view, I stepped to the microphone. "Ladies and gentlemen, this is the regular Saturday evening street meeting for Evangel Temple. I believe that at this time it would be appropriate to sing 'God Save the Queen.' " And with that, I hit the trumpet and Norma-Jean accompanied on the accordion, and all up and down the street, the crowd stood to attention and began to sing, "God save our gracious Queen." She smiled and waved as she passed by, and I wondered if she ever had had it happen quite like that before.

As soon as the last strains of the anthem died away, and with the motorcade now out of sight, I said, "Ladies and gentlemen, we have just given great attention to the Queen of the British Commonwealth. Now I'm going to ask you to give five minutes' attention while I tell you about the King of kings who will one day visit Brighton."

In that five minutes, I preached an evangelistic message like I had never preached before. There were quite a few new faces in our church the next morning, and I made a special point of thanking all of those in our congregation whose intercessory prayers had made the whole thing possible. Without those prayers, that whole extraordinary episode might never have happened; the Queen might have simply passed through at six o'clock instead of seven.

The street meetings continued through the summer, but with the coming of fall and colder weather, we had to come up with an alternative plan. What came to me was the idea to have youth rallies. There were just over two thousand people in Brighton, but in the surrounding area there were ten churches, and all of them had young people who had nothing to do on Saturday night. We organized joint youth rallies in which all the churches participated. These were a tremendous success.

Many lives were changed that year, but probably no individual's experience was as moving as that of Dr. Bradley Stewart. There were only three doctors in Brighton, and Dr. Stewart, who was married to a former

Miss Toronto and had five children, was assistant to the chief surgeon at Trenton Hospital. There was tremendous pressure in his job and his life, and he had tried to cope with them through alcohol and drugs to which he had instant and unlimited access. By the time we moved to Brighton, his practice had largely diminished as had his income.

Matters came to a head one morning, when he showed up for work with such a hangover that he was barred from the operating room, and it was made clear to him that he was very close to losing his license to practice medicine. That afternoon he went to a golf club in Trenton, where he enjoyed buying drinks for the other men, and he drank even more than his usual amount. Driving home, he ran off the road and into the ditch, hitting a telephone pole and demolishing his car. Miraculously, he was unhurt.

Constable Summers, whose father was a deacon in my church, was the first officer on the scene. He picked Dr. Stewart up out of the ditch, and as he did so, the doctor turned and swung at him. That earned the doctor a night in jail, and it came out that he could not afford to put up his own bail, but had to ask for help from a friend. When he got home, his wife and children were gone, and there was a note on the hall table: "The only communication you'll receive from me will be through my lawyer."

By this time, Dr. Stewart was cold sober—and very distraught. He called the minister of his church, where he had served as an official, but his minister, who had counseled him fruitlessly for countless hours and even taken him to AA meetings, said that he was sorry, but there was nothing further he could do to help him. In desperation, the doctor then called me. "Rev. Mainse, Mrs. Edwards and Mrs. Ball of your congregation have been my patients, and I've seen physical miracles in their lives, things that medicine cannot explain. They told me that over at your church, you'd prayed for them, and they were healed. I need a miracle in my own life now—could you come over and pray for me?"

I told him I would be tied up for a while, but I could come over after that, around eleven.

"That's wonderful," he said, greatly relieved, "but, um, would you mind parking your car down the street a bit?" I told him I wouldn't mind, and smiled to myself; in spite of all that had happened to him, he did not consider himself as low on the scale as the Pentecostal minister.

When I got there, he took me into his office, and we had hardly sat down, when he said, "Before you try to convert me, I want to tell you that I believe Christ came and died for my sins, and I even believe in the Virgin Birth." Apparently he expected me to be stunned. "But it has made no difference in my life."

Well, Lord, what do I do now? I glanced at the wall behind him. His various degrees were all nicely framed there—the University of Toronto Faculty of Medicine, the special certificate in surgery, a picture of his graduating class and several other mementos.

I thought for a moment, then said, "I believe you are every bit as fully qualified a doctor as those degrees attest. What's more, I believe you are a kind one, as well as a good one. I know poor people in this town whom you've never billed, and you've helped them tremendously. I believe all that." I paused and looked him in the eye. "But I don't believe in you."

He was taken aback. "What do you mean?" he managed.

"I believe *about* you, but I don't believe *in* you. I have never had to put my life in your hands. I have never been about to take an anesthetic before being put on the operating table, totally yielded and surrendered to you, knowing that in a few minutes, when I was unconscious, you would take a knife and cut me open and operate on me. So I believe about you, but I've never had to believe in you."

He looked at me, and for a long time neither of us spoke. I could see it was dawning on him that he had believed all the right doctrines about Jesus, but he had never believed *in* Him, to the point of trusting Him unconditionally with his life.

I asked him if he would like to pray. He nodded and abruptly slipped off the couch onto his knees. "O God, I give you my life, just as totally as the person on the operating table gives me theirs. I yield to you, Lord, and give you permission to do whatever needs to be done in me. Operate on me, Lord; I believe in you. I believe in you," he repeated, and the tears came freely.

The next Sunday he came to our church and stood and wept again, as he publicly thanked Mrs. Edwards and Mrs. Ball for sharing what God had done in their lives. One of the ushers, noting that the back door was ajar, went to close it, and discovered Clive Thompson, the town lawyer who was also the organist from Dr. Stewart's church, standing outside, listening. Their service had finished earlier, and he couldn't believe Dr. Stewart was in there, and had come to see for himself.

In a town as small as Brighton, everyone knows everyone else's business, and the town was shaken by the transformation in Dr.

76

Stewart's life. But his reputation had been so badly eroded that starting over was almost impossible; also his debts had taken everything he had, even his instruments. But God began to move. Some of the doctor's Christian neighbors came from a little town north of Kingston. The town's doctor had just died, and the town, hearing Dr. Stewart's story, was prepared to build an office for him, and the deceased doctor's sister donated his instruments. They were even prepared to set him up in a residence, if his wife and children would come back to him.

Christmas time was approaching, and Dr. Stewart desperately wanted to be reunited with his family, but he had no idea where his wife was. She had family in Toronto, yet the phone there did not answer, and so the two of us went to Toronto together. He had been served with divorce papers, and the trial was coming up in January, but she had refused all communication from him. When we got to Toronto, we had no idea where to begin looking and we simply prayed. It came to me that it was Christmas time and the stores would be hiring extra help; why not start there?

The first store we walked into was Eaton's downtown store on College Street, and there, behind the lingerie counter, was his wife. As soon as she saw him, she turned and walked away, but I went to her. "Cathy, God has done a miracle in your husband's life."

"I'm sorry, but I don't believe it!" She was about to turn away from me too, but I pleaded with her to at least let me drive her home when she finished work. "All right," she said finally, "but I don't want him anywhere around." That evening I picked her up and shared Christ with her in her home. She wouldn't make any commitments; she was reserving judgment. But when the case came up in court in January, instead of her lawyer appearing, she came herself, and agreed to a reconciliation.

Some months later, I received a phone call. "David, it's Brad. I just wanted to call and let you know how things are going. It hasn't been easy, but we're all together, and it's working. I keep a Bible on my desk, and I find that most of the people who come in here don't need pills or treatments; they need the Word of God. They need Jesus. I can't always share Him with them, of course; I have to wait until I sense the Lord's leading. But I have been able to share Him with a surprising number of my patients."

Three days after that phone call, Brad Stewart died of heart failure at thirty-nine years of age. God had forgiven his sins, but his body hadn't. He had been driving himself day and night and his heart finally gave out. I learned he had been using his station wagon as an ambulance, since Verona had no ambulance service, and he had received an award for heroism. He had been driving a pregnant woman to the hospital to have her baby, and along the way they passed a house on fire. Dr. Stewart had stopped, gone into the flaming building, and rescued three people, and then taken the pregnant lady to the hospital. His life as a Christian may have been short, but he had made it count, and I am looking forward to seeing him in heaven.

A year later, our second daughter, Ellen, was born, and not long after that, I got some very disturbing news from Chalk River. The young couple whom the district had put in the church there and had supported with home mission funds had left the work on short notice, and the church had closed again. Once more, the Lord seemed to lay an aching burden on my heart for those people, and the more I prayed for them, the stronger the burden became.

Ultimately, I knew I would have to put a call in to W.B. Greenwood, the district superintendent. I didn't want to; I was only twenty-four years old and had been in my present position less than three years. But from the unceasing agitation in my heart, I knew I would have no peace unless I called him.

CHAPTER 10

Return to Chalk River

Rev. Greenwood remembered my devotion to the people of Chalk River; in fact, he had already been wondering if I might be considering returning to that area. "But, David," he said when I made no secret of my joy at this prospect, "the district executive committee feels that there needs to be a broader base to support a minister with a family. They feel that they should go into Deep River, six miles away, with its five thousand people, as opposed to Chalk River, with its twelve hundred. Also this time, we're going to buy land and build, to let people know in no uncertain terms that this assembly will be there to stay."

The property was found, and a contractor was approached for an estimate. The sum he came up with was $30,000, a substantial amount in those days, and it was raised by my giving notes to people who would make personal loans, with the Pentecostal Assemblies of Eastern Ontario and Quebec, some one hundred churches, standing behind it, as if it were a mission church. Construction was slated to begin in the fall, and I started scouting for every available source of help.

I had no congregation to call on; of the original group, there was a remaining nucleus of four women and one man who was on unemployment. But Tom and Betty Charbonneau, who had moved to Pembroke, came to help us, as did several other families who had once been with us. A remarkable number of skilled workmen from other churches pitched in simply because they wanted to. Norma-Jean and I were renting down in Pembroke, twenty-seven miles away. We couldn't find even temporary accommodations in Deep River.

I would leave home very early and arrive on the sight by seven in the morning, and would get back home at ten or eleven at night, spending the day helping the men who were volunteering their time. The pressure on our lives at that time was intense, and twice I had taken Norma-Jean to the hospital at Trenton, with what turned out to be false labor. Finally, a week after we arrived in Pembroke, the labor pains were for real. In those days, nurses treated expectant fathers as if they had perpetrated some mysterious crime on expectant mothers, and I was left to sit for hours uninformed in the waiting room.

Fortunately, a close Christian friend of ours, Dr. Arnold Faught, came into the hospital just about the time I thought I heard a newborn baby cry. "Arnold!" I exclaimed. "Thank God, you've come! I think that might be my baby I hear crying in the delivery room, but they won't let me anywhere near it. Could you go and see if everything's all right?"

He went and poked his head in, and returned a moment later, swaggering with a big grin. I grinned back; I knew Norma-Jean had just given birth to our first son. But it was not an easy delivery. The poor, wee lad had to be turned with forceps while he was still in the womb. And then he picked up a staph infection somewhere in the hospital and broke out in boils which he suffered from, on and off, for more than a year. The infection would seem to disappear, only to break out again a few days later, and the boils were very painful to little Reynold.

The construction was progressing ahead of schedule, and I loved every minute of it. When there was a carpenter available, I was the carpenter's helper. I was the plumber's assistant on plumbing jobs, and the laborer who put up the scaffolding and heaved the twelve-inch blocks up to the men who were laying them. When the job was finished in December, I was almost sorry; I was in the best physical shape of my life. We had a friend named Cecil Krieger in Pembroke who was a building contractor, and he turned his crew over to us asking only that we pay them at his cost price. Cecil also gave us the materials at his cost, so that when all the figures were in, we brought the job in for $15,000—excatly half of what it had been estimated at!

An apartment had been built for our family in the basement of the church. It measured ten feet by fifty feet, about the size of a large trailer, and we loved it. Norma-Jean especially liked the kitchen, in which I had built every conceivable type of cabinet. At that time, I was receiving a salary of twenty-five dollars a week, barely enough for subsistence. We regarded the work as a mission field, and it never occurred to us to expect anything more.

On January 28, 1962, we dedicated the new Calvary Church, and those first two weeks, I brought in two guest speakers, Dr. Harry Faught of the Danforth Gospel Temple in Toronto, and Rev. Robert Argue, from the Montreal Evangel Church, which had provided all our chairs. They got us off to a glorious start, and our attendance increased every Sunday after that.

Recalling my leading in Chalk River seven years before, I set myself the goal of knocking on the front door of every house in Deep River. It was a forbidding prospect, in a sense, because Deep River, with its vast atomic energy complex, was the residential area for the greatest concentration of scientific brain power in the country. I was about to approach men whom modern society, in its worship of technology as the solution to man's problems, had elevated to the status of gods. A status, incidentally, which the scientists themselves were somewhat reluctant to set aside. Lately, of course, the illusion of technology as the universal solution has been largely seen to be bankrupt, but this was seventeen years ago, and back in '62, the dream was still intact.

Needless to say, the message I brought fell for the most part upon deaf ears. But it was something I had to do, and it did bring forth fruit. For instance, one scientist with whom I spoke had three sons, approximately six, eight, and ten years old. I mentioned the possibility of the boys attending Sunday school and he said, "I'm not going to let you get them there and brainwash them." I started to reply, but he went on. "When they get old enough to make up their own minds, then they will make their own decision whether or not to be Christians."

"But is that a fair test? Are you being objective in giving them only one side of the story from which to make an intelligent decision?" I asked, appealing to the scientific side of his nature. He thought about that and admitted that they would get no exposure to the Christian position at public school or in his home. And he agreed to let them come to Sunday school. But to be sure that his sons would not be brainwashed, he himself sat in on their Sunday school classes for several weeks—until he apparently got too embarrassed to continue, and went upstairs to join the adults.

So it was that he was in the congregation Easter Sunday morning, when we had the most joyous service of our first year. There must have been eighty or ninety people present; nearly every seat was taken. That morning George and Marilyn Laronde, one of the first couples to give their lives to Christ in our new church, had asked if their two children could be dedicated to Jesus, and now they brought them forward. As I prepared to dedicate them, George said to me, "Pastor, could you also pray for Timmy's foot? He was born with no heel bone in his left foot."

I was holding Timmy in my arms, and as George spoke, I could feel it was true: there was no heel on the little foot, and it was turned inward. Before answering, I sought God in my heart, and the spirit of prophecy came upon me. I said to the congregation: "This is Easter Sunday morning, and if Christ is indeed risen from the dead, He will do the things for people today that He did when He walked the earth in mortal flesh."

I dedicated Timmy to the Lord, and then said, "Now we're going to pray for Timmy, and Jesus is going to prove He's alive. Either He's alive, or He's dead, and the soldiers were right when they said that while they slept, the disciples came and stole away the body. Let's believe God." Part of me was startled at the boldness of this challenge, but I went ahead and prayed for Timmy. Then I felt his foot again; I could feel no difference. Nevertheless, I proclaimed, "When this child is old enough to walk, he will walk normally."

A few days later, Timmy's mother, Marilyn, burst into our apartment with her son in her arms. "Look at Timmy's foot!" she cried. "Just look!" His left foot had straightened around, and the heel bone had come into place. Timmy walked earlier than his older sister had, and today he has two perfectly normal feet, and plays hockey and does all the other things a boy of seventeen does.

Not long after this, the United Church down in Chalk River was moving into larger quarters, and their old building was for sale. I wrote to the moderator of the United Church about it, and he wrote a letter to that congregation, encouraging them to sell us the building. The price was certainly right, $2500, and we bought it and renovated it and commenced having afternoon services in it. I was thrilled. Chalk River had always been my first love, and now those people, who were a decidedly different sort than the folks of Deep River, and who had originally come to the Orange Hall at last would have a church of their own.

Our young people took on the project of buying a Sunday school bus, because there was no Sunday school north of us. When we got it, I would get up early on Sundays and drive forty-four miles north to Deux

Rivieres, to bus children in. After church, one of my deacons would drive them back, while I had lunch. He would arrive just as I finished the last, hasty bite of dessert, and he wouldn't even turn the engine off. We'd swap off, and then I would take the bus and pick up children on the way to the Chalk River service in the afternoon. All told, between the two churches, we must have had about 165 young people in Sunday school.

To help us properly launch the Chalk River church, I asked Ralph Rutledge to come up and take a week of meetings there, which he did. At one of those meetings, the wife of Ken, the scientist with the three sons, came forward and knelt at the altar and wept and invited Christ into her life. The following Sunday, Ken himself was in the congregation, and I noticed, as I gave an invitation for people to come to Christ and we sang the invitational hymn, that his face became very red. He seemed quite agitated, and all of a sudden he made a beeline for the altar rail and began to pray.

Afterwards, I asked Ken what had happened. He said he had been moved by the service and what had happened to his wife a few nights before, and as we were singing the invitational hymn, he prayed, "O God, if you're real, you know how I have to have everything proven in a test tube. So, if you're real, do something. Let me feel you." As he prayed that, something came over him, from the crown of his head right on down, something that felt like pins and needles, though not unpleasantly so. When it came over him, he began to feel increasing heat, and he cried aloud and knew he had to get to the altar and give his life to Christ. Ken is out in Calgary now, and I haven't heard from him lately, but I suspect there is a Bible tucked among all the technical books in his office.

It was about this time, in the early summer of '62, that the Lord opened a new dimension in our ministry—one that would have far-reaching ramifications in the future, that we could not even dream of, but when it first happened, it was in passing, almost by accident.

It all began with the return of Norma-Jean's two brothers, Glen and Reynold, and Bob Ostrosser, from Australia. They and three other men had formed a gospel singing group called the King's Men, and this group had been challenged to go down to Australia, to help start a Christian summer ranch program for teenagers. They took their families with them, selling everything they owned to pay their way, and spent two years at this project. They worked in a chain of appliance stores during the day, and gave concerts at night, and when they left, they had gotten the pilot ranch off to a good start. (Today, there are eighteen such ranches, throughout Australia, New Zealand, and Indonesia.)

While they were down under, I had written Reyn and Glen and asked them for a week of meetings in our new church, as soon as they got home. What I did not realize was that they had cut a gospel record which had risen high on the Australian music charts, so that they had gained something of celebrity status when they got home. We decided to get as much publicity for their week of meetings as we possibly could, and so, armed with copies of their record, I went to the nearest radio station, which was in Pembroke, and got them to play it. And then, on an impulse, I drove back down to Pembroke, where the nearest and newest television station was.

I told the owner and general manager of the station, Gordon Archibald, about the King's Men and their record, and the week's meetings they would be having at our church in Deep River. They had a policy that there would be no gospel broadcasting on their television station, but he had heard the King's Men record on the local radio station, and agreed that I could do a show with them as my guests. But he warned me not to use the opportunity to launch into a full-scale sermon. That was fine; what I had in mind was a fifteen-minute slot somewhere, with me talking a little about the gospel and featuring the King's Men and their hit songs. It might stir up some extra interest in our forthcoming meetings.

Something seemed to click between me and Gordon, because he said he could make such a slot for us, by delaying the Saturday night late movie fifteen minutes after the late news and sports, which were over at 11:30. And the cost would be only fifty-five dollars. *Only* fifty-five dollars—that was more than two weeks' salary! But I had a good witness in my spirit, and sensed God's go-ahead, and so, trusting Him for the funds, I agreed. And, actually, the timing couldn't have been better. Back in 1962, television was just making its way up into northern Ontario, and the entire province was responding like a kid with a new toy. Television antennas were sprouting up on rooftops everywhere, and since there was only one late movie a week in those days, everyone stayed up to watch it.

As the night of the telecast approached, I grew increasingly nervous. It was ridiculous, of course; hadn't I preached in the streets to hundreds?

Yes, replied the voice that was harassing me, but now you will be going into the living rooms of thousands. Total strangers, in the comfort of their living rooms or bedrooms, will be observing you with skeptical curiosity. And you will be going out live: that means no editing—any bloopers are going to be right out there.

When that Saturday night in May arrived, as Glen and Reynold and I waited on the studio's little sound stage, watching the nightly news as it was being piped in from Toronto on the monitor set, my anxiety reached the level of low-grade panic. The studio clock's big hand was falling fast towards 11:30, its sweep-second hand accelerating at a dizzying pace. We were supposed to be in prayer, and Reyn and Glen, who had done a lot of broadcasting in Australia, seemed to be relaxed enough, I thought, a trifle enviously.

Finally, I was able to quiet down inside to the point where I could calmly pray. I could hear Him. His solution, as usual, was so simple that I had overlooked it: talk to Ted Wheeler. Ted lived in Deep River, and he had a drinking problem that was about to ruin his marriage and destroy his family. I had recently met him as part of my door-to-door visiting campaign, and he had promised to watch tonight's program. So, instead of looking into a cold camera lens, I imagined him sitting there in his living room in his undershirt, a half-consumed case of beer by his chair, and an open bottle in his hand. I imagined myself sitting on the sofa in his living room, sharing with him on a one-to-one basis, and all the nervousness left. When the red light went on and we were on the air, I was able to minister in the same anointing of the Holy Spirit, as if I were visiting him in person, or preaching in the pulpit.

The King's Men sang beautifully, and played trombone, marimba, and piano. I made a brief but forceful presentation of the gospel of Jesus Christ. When the show was over, the station manager was ecstatic. "Look at our switchboard out there! It's jammed with calls! People are calling long-distance to tell us how much they enjoyed your broadcast. We've never had a response like this to anything we've broadcast!" And when he calmed down, he said, "I want you to come on again, anytime you have a singing group like the King's Men. In fact, we will make the same fifteen-minute slot available to you on a regular weekly basis for fifty-five dollars a week."

But the most gratifying result of these broadcasts came at 5:00 A.M., Sunday morning. The phone rang, and I groped my way out of a deep sleep and eventually got the receiver to my ear. "Hello, David, this is Ted."

"Huh?"

"Ted Wheeler."

"You drunk, Ted?"

"Nope, cold sober. That's what I'm calling about." I began to wake up. "I watched that show last night. I felt like you were talking just to me. I tried to get to sleep afterward, but I tossed and turned till about 4:00 A.M., and finally I couldn't take it any more. I got out of bed and got on my knees, and I called on God to save my soul and save my life and save my family." His voice began to crack with emotion. "I know God has heard me, and that I'm a new person. I know I've been born again."

That morning, Ted came to church, and he testified of what had happened to him.

And that was how our TV ministry began. In the beginning, I asked my old Bible college and traveling buddy, Ralph Rutledge, and his wife, Evelyn, to appear with Norma-Jean and me on the show. Since it was a live telecast, we needed to be at the little studio well in advance of air-time in order to rehearse our songs and the format of the program, and usually we were. But there was one Saturday in which we had been down at our teen camp on Round Lake, which was twenty-five miles south of Pembroke, on the border of Algonquin Park.

Our wives were already in Pembroke on this particular evening, and we had arranged to meet them at a particular street corner, at a particular time. In the meantime, Ralph and I were on the road, driving north, in the middle of nowhere, when all of a sudden the car began to gasp and buck and die. We were out of gas, and miles from a station. It was dark, and time was critical, and as we sat silently in the car, it seemed that the night sounds of the crickets and other things were very loud.

Finally, Ralph broke the silence. "Do you hear what I hear?"

"Obviously," I said, angry, and ready to make him the scapegoat. "What do you hear?"

"Look, Ralph, it's ten-thirty. We were supposed to be picking the girls up fifteen minutes ago, and you're asking me what I hear? I hear grasshoppers and crickets and other bugs. Now what—"

"Don't you hear the water?" And now that he mentioned it, I did hear running water. Switching the lights back on, I saw that we had come to rest almost directly over a culvert, through which a little creek flowed.

"Okay, I hear the water, so what?"

"Well, Jesus turned water into wine, and I heard that this same thing once happened to our old friend, Rev. R.E. Sternall. He put water in his gas tank and prayed for the Lord to turn it into gasoline, and He did."

"Well, I believe in prayer, and I know it is only going to be God's mercy that gets us out of here, but if you think I'm going to put creek water in my gas tank—"

"David, why don't we try it and believe that God will change it? Otherwise, we're not going to make it."

"Well, let's wait until we have *your* car and then try it, okay?"

And just then a car came along, and both of us prayed like mad that he would stop, and he did. He took us to the next gas station, where they loaned us a gas can and gave us a ride back. We got the car going, filled it up at the station, and got to the studio at 11:27! Norma-Jean and Evelyn were so relieved to see us, they weren't even angry! And from all reports, it was one of our best shows.

One other thing that happened that summer was the drive-in church we organized for Sunday evenings. Actually, it was an idea derived from the Saturday night street meetings in Brighton. For all those people who are unlikely ever to go to church on their own, why not take the church to them? I made arrangements with the owner of the shopping plaza in Deep River to bring a truck with an organ and sound equipment to his parking lot on Sunday evenings at seven. And with the help of our young people, that is what we did.

It was about as informal a setting as you could ever imagine for a church; people came in shorts, in bathing suits and sandals, whatever they happened to be wearing. We would have a regular service, only instead of having a perspiring group in a sweltering church, we had hundreds, dressed casually and sitting in the comfort of their cars. Around eight o'clock, I would give the invitation, and people would get out of their cars and come forward. If they wanted personal prayer or counseling, instead of raising their hands as they might in church, they would turn on their lights, and our young soul-winners would move around among their cars. Then, at 8:15 I would jump in the cab of the truck and drive to Camp Petawawa, and repeat the service at the shopping plaza there.

One Sunday evening, towards the end of the summer, it had been raining, and though it had stopped, dark thunderclouds loomed ominously, promising a resumption of the downpour at any moment. And from the look of the sky, it was sure to be a deluge. The gentleman who owned the plaza, a Jewish man who always smoked a cigar, had lately taken to coming over to our services himself, his long black Cadillac parked discretely on the periphery. On this particular night, as we were setting up our sound equipment, he strolled over. "Doesn't look like you're going to be able to preach tonight, Rev," he said, smiling around the cigar.

"Oh, yes, we will," I said, smiling back.

"Nope," he shook his head, "it's going to rain cats and dogs here any minute."

"We'll see," I replied, taking the tarpaulin off of the organ. That organ was our church's pride and joy, and I noticed a couple of the deacons looking at me askance; if that organ got wet, it would be ruined.

I opened the service by declaring, "Either the God of Elijah," and here I glanced over at our Jewish benefactor, "is alive today, or He's dead. If He is alive, then He is the same, and He's just waiting for someone to call upon Him, as Elijah did in the days of old. Elijah prayed that it would not rain, and God held back the rain for three-and-a-half years. Well, Lord, we're not asking for that long; just about an hour would do fine," and everyone laughed. "So, rain," I exclaimed, pointing at the darkening heavens, "you just stay up there in the sky until we're finished!"

All through the service, it got blacker and blacker, and though we were still a good two hours from sunset, the storm clouds made it so dark that the drivers of the cars on the highway had to turn on their lights. More and more it looked like rain—it even smelled like rain—but we didn't hurry. We gave the invitation, and people got out of their cars and came forward to receive Christ. I pronounced the benediction, pulled the tarp over the organ, and climbed into the cab of the truck. The instant the cab door closed, the heavens opened. The rain came down so hard, it was like someone had tilted a huge basin over. Even with the wipers going full speed, I could barely see.

Just then, I noticed a long black shadow looming up alongside. It was the Cadillac, and the driver had put down the window on the passenger side of his car; he wanted to say something. I cranked down my own window, getting half soaked in the process. Our Jewish friend grinned up at me and shouted, "You got something there, boy! Stick with it!" And with that, his window went up, and he was gone.

By the beginning of the following summer, 1964, I began to notice a stirring within me that I had come to recognize; God was getting ready to move me. Both our churches were thriving, and we were already at work on expanding the Deep River facility. But if God *was* about to move us, I had to ask Him for four things. First, I prayed that it would be a city of at least a hundred thousand where there would be real potential for growth and development, where a church could grow to the point that it could support a missionary program. Second, I prayed that it would be to a church where we could continue the TV ministry and begin to branch out to other stations, and where the church board would be willing to back us up in this ministry. Third, for the sake of my family, I asked for it to be a church that could afford to pay us more than twenty-five dollars weekly, so we wouldn't have to always be praying in enough extra money to keep groceries on the table and clothes on our children. And finally, for Norma-Jean's sake, I hoped it would be a church with a nice parsonage.

All of which was, of course, in the event that God did move us. I was not insisting on moving, by any means. I loved where I was. But I had this stirring, and I had known it before.

But when the phone call came, it came so completely out of the blue, I couldn't have been more surprised.

David Charles Mainse,
age 9 months, 1937.

David at age 2
with Elaine, Willa,
mother and dad.

A *The young schoolboy in 1944.*
B *The threshold of manhood—David at 15.*
C *Annesley College—1946.*

Norma-Jean, David and Dad Mainse, 1958.

Orange Hall—Chalk River,
Ont., 1956.

Parsonage interior,
Chalk River, Ont., 1956.

Deep River Church, 1962.

The wedding.

New pastor and family, Bethel Tabernacle,
Hamilton, Ont., 1968.

Sudbury—Channel 5—CKSO-TV, 1964-1967.

Behind the scenes.

100 Huntley Street.

Lily Farquhar, Bunny Martin, John Wallace
and Mike Cassidy—mail room staff.

Camera crew members—Tim Moorehead, Eleanore Lannin
and Bob Wells—share an impromptu prayer.

Jesus' joy is contagious.

David with Bob MacDougall in action.

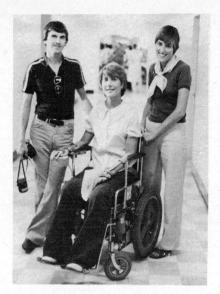

Joni at 100 Huntley Street shares
break time with Bruce and Moira Allen.

Champion boxer, George Forman,
on the set with Bob MacDougall.

Evie Tornquist visits—June, 1978.

David and Pat Robertson talking shop.

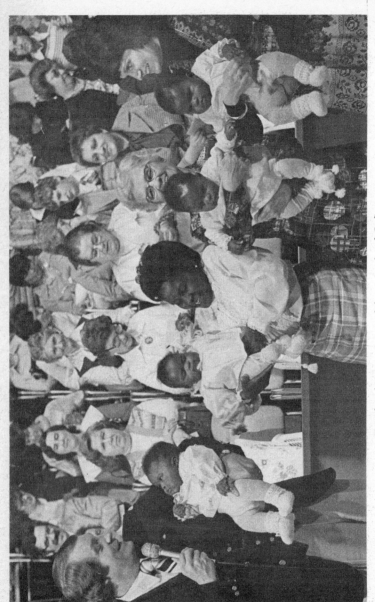

David and Norma-Jean and four miracles of God's grace.

Norma-Jean ministers joy!

"Crossroads" set.

Circle Square.

A word in season.

The team—Norma-Jean and David.

The life line—100 Huntley Street.

The heart of the matter.

CHAPTER 11

Crossroads

"Did you say Sudbury, operator?" Sudbury was a large mining city, the nickel capital of the world, about five hours north of Toronto. I had never been there, and knew no one from there. The phone call was from Homer Cantelon, pastor of the Glad Tidings Tabernacle; he wanted me to come and preach for a call. As he was being called away, and they would soon be in need of a pastor, he and the deacons felt that God would have them approach me.

So, one sunny morning, I drove up there. From Deep River, it was another 180 miles northwest, and as I neared the city, it looked like its population was a good 100,000. Some of the territory on the outskirts of the city was so barren that NASA actually brought its future moon astronauts there to familiarize them with conditions they could expect on the moon. But the city itself was clean and seemed to have an atmosphere of caring. The church looked like it held around two hundred, and it was nicely full. Right away, I sensed the unity and love of the congregation.

After the service, the deacons invited me to have a talk with them. I spoke frankly, and told them of my commitment to the television ministry, adding that in any call I might consider, it would have to be given priority. That night, the congregation voted to issue me a call, and the next time I met with the deacons, they said they were prepared to pick up our television expenses until such time as sufficient financial support was coming in from our viewers, but they could not do so for more than three months. The clincher came three days later, when the owner of the Pembroke TV station, where it had all begun, wrote to the manager of the station in Sudbury. "I understand that David Mainse may be moving to your city. This young fellow has had a weekly TV program here which has been extremely successful, and which the people in our area have much appreciated. If you are able to help him produce his program, please send us a tape of it, as we would like to continue showing it on Saturday nights at 11:30." The Sudbury manager agreed.

That settled it; we moved in August of '64. There were six of us now, for God had given us another son, Ronald, a little over a year earlier. The new production facilities in Sudbury were considerably more sophisticated—and expensive—than those we had been accustomed to, but we sensed that God was still very much with us, and so we trusted Him to meet our financial commitments. All we needed now was a name, and after a good deal of thought, and even more prayer, we named the program, "Crossroads."

The Lord did provide our financial needs, but not as completely as we had hoped. With the three months almost up, we were still running short of what we needed. In desperation I asked the Lord if there was anything we should be doing. As I listened, He seemed to lead me to the first chapter of Paul's letter to Philippi, as it appears in the Amplified Bible. Reading it, I was particularly struck by the fifth verse: "[I thank my God] for your fellowship—your sympathetic cooperation and contributions and partnership—in advancing the good news (the Gospel) from the first day [you heard it] until now." There was something there—particularly in that amplification of the word "fellowship": *sympathetic cooperation and contributions and partnership*.

And then I had it—of course! We would invite sympathetic individuals to enter into partnership with us. As we made "Crossroads" available to them as a witnessing tool, we would ask them to become prayer partners with us, and those who could, to consider making monthly contributions, in addition to supporting us in prayer. We would call them Cooperators—co-operators in Operation Crossroads. I printed up some pledge cards and took them around to friends, and in this way, we met our budget in time. It was a concept, well-used over the years, which would see its greatest use more than a dozen years in the future.

One other concept which the Lord gave me in those early days in Sudbury did not come into use at all, for at least that long. I had been praying about "Crossroads," and what changes in format the Lord might like to see, when I got a picture in my mind's eye of telephones, with people calling in, right while we were on the air, to commit their lives to Christ, or to ask for healing. I grew very excited about the possibility. What if someone could just call the studio and tell a counselor what had happened in his or her heart? What if they wanted to pray the sinner's prayer and accept Jesus into their hearts, and just wanted someone to lead them?

I went to the television management with the concept, and they gave it serious consideration, but decided it would simply be too expensive to do the show live, which it obviously had to be, and to run all those phone lines into the studio. Their decision was that "Crossroads" would have to continue to be videotaped in advance, and that was that. (A year later, Pat Robertson was to stage the miraculous telethon he describes in *Shout It From the Housetops,* out of which eventually emerged the concept of a live phone-in program: the "700 Club.")

But a curious thing happened almost immediately after their negative decision. A United Church minister in Sudbury, named Bruce MacDougall, told about a telephone outreach in Australia, initiated by Dr. Alan Walker of Sydney. It was called "Life-Line," and what it amounted to was a twenty-four-hour Christian crisis center. Well, maybe *that* was the phone ministry God had been speaking to me about. I threw my weight behind the proposal, got our people involved in becoming counselors in Sudbury's own version of "Life-Line," and the idea took hold. Today, it is called "Telecare," and has spread from Sudbury all across North America.

Now God began to expand the outreach of "Crossroads." A pastor in Sault Ste. Marie saw the program and went to his local TV station to see what it would cost to make "Crossroads" available there each week. It was within reason, and soon the program had a third outlet. Then Timmins wanted it, and North Bay and Quebec City. Syndication continued to expand; "Crossroads" became the first gospel TV program to be seen in the great urban metropolises of Canada—Montreal, Toronto, and Vancouver. As the months went by, and more stations came on the line, our costs naturally escalated, and our board of deacons was becoming very concerned. We were meeting our budget through contributions, yet they were feeling the weight of the responsibility for the program's affairs being run in good order.

Tom Johnstone, general superintendent of the Pentecostal Assemblies of Canada, put together a committee, which included himself, Don Feltmate and Albert Vaters, among others, to meet with our board of deacons. The committee offered to lift responsibility for overseeing the finances and the administration of the TV ministry from the hands of the local church, by forming a national board of directors of "Crossroads," to which two of our deacons were appointed. I couldn't have been happier.

Although from the beginning our broadcasts have been nondenominational in format and will remain so, I am grateful to have the board of directors looking over my shoulder at our monthly balance sheets, to make sure everything is done properly and in order. Their authority has always been a confidence-builder, and it certainly comes in handy when someone calls in and starts making allegations.

In the meantime, my pastoral duties kept me fully occupied. The third Sunday evening that I preached at Glad Tidings, God laid a strong evangelistic message on my heart. But as I started to speak, I didn't feel like I was getting anywhere. So I simply stopped, and then asked them: "How many of you know the Lord?" Every hand went up. No wonder I was having difficulty! But what of my leading—had I not heard God, after all? I stood there, wondering, while the congregation sat there, also wondering. Through the open window, I could hear the strains of music and the sound of occasional outbursts of raucous laughter coming down the alley. That was the Mine Mill Hall, where they were having a dance. It was the union hall, and it was known to be a tough place that had very little use for the things of God.

I knew what I had to do. Calling one of the deacons to the pulpit, I told him the Lord had given me an evangelistic message, and I was bound to deliver one, and to people who didn't already know the Lord Jesus. I said to the congregation, "I have to leave now. You folks can leave also, or you can go to the prayer room and pray," and I left the deacon in the pulpit and walked out. I never did hear what he did; he probably called the people to prayer, to pray for this crazy new pastor they had.

Walking down the alley, and across the street to the Mine Mill Hall, I found a crowd of about a hundred or so, which had overflowed from the hall, and had gathered sociably on its front steps. My heart leapt at the sight, for had I tried to go inside, I would surely have been thrown out. Now I wouldn't have to; I could stand on the sidewalk, which was city property, and there were more than enough people to speak to, right there. So I did. And that night, out of that crowd, two men came to know the Lord.

As I was talking with people afterwards, I noticed out of the corner of my eye, two of our deacons were driving slowly by, nonplussed at what they saw their new pastor up to. Oh, well, we would get used to one another in time. And as it happened, we never had another Sunday evening service in which we did not have at least some people present who did not know the Lord.

Glad Tidings was full when I got there, and it grew even more crowded as our attendance climbed by roughly a quarter in the first few months. There were no two ways about it; we had to build. With the unanimous support of the deacons and consent of the congregation, we commenced a building program.

This time, our needs were much greater than they had been in Deep River—and so was our estimate, $250,000! It was decided that we would act as our own contractor, and encourage volunteer labor. From the experience I had gained at Deep River, it was felt I should do the buying of material. I planned to spend every daylight hour on the site working at whatever needed to be done, to encourage the volunteers but also because I just plain enjoyed physical labor.

I have always felt that if you can put a church on the main thoroughfare of a city, it multiplies the impact of your newspaper or other advertising three or four times, because everyone knows immediately where that church is. In Sudbury, there is a rocky promontory that juts up out of the heart of the city. We were able to purchase property at the top of this outcropping, which meant our church would be visible for miles. The architect created a church for us that was modern and yet entirely compatible with its surroundings; it looked like it grew right out of the rock precipice that towered over Regent Street.

Our goal was to finish the church by 1967, Canada's Centennial, and thus it became, in a sense, a Centennial project for the whole city. People came from all over to help; many didn't even know the Lord, but had heard we were taking on the project and they had a skill to offer. The first thing that needed to be done, of course, was to blast into the rock base with pneumatic drills, to pour the concrete footings that would support the building. It made a tremendous racket, but it got the job done, and I took my turn using these drills.

One time, there were a couple of other fellows using the drills in the evening, and they had gotten so enthusiastic that they hadn't noticed dusk had fallen. Finally, a policeman had to come and tell them it was eleven o'clock, and people were complaining of the noise.

But an episode I remember most vividly concerning those footings occurred towards the end of that summer of '66. I was drilling about fifteen feet below the roadway to which the front door would one day open, and where I had parked the car. Taking a break to stretch, I looked up and noticed Reyn and Ron, whom I had brought with me, both crying their eyes out. I climbed up to see what was the matter, but they were too heartsick to answer. Finally Reyn, who was about four, managed to point to a cliff at the other side of the roadway. All of a sudden I thought, "Where's the car?"

I ran to the edge of the cliff where Reyn was pointing, and there, about twenty-five feet down a fairly steep incline, was our 1965 Ford station wagon, the only new car we had ever owned, with the front end pretty badly smashed in. What was more, I had a number of the heavy steel drill bits in the back of the wagon, and these came crashing into the front, when the car hit bottom.

It was obvious what had happened: somehow, the boys had managed to get into the car, take the emergency brake off and get it out of park, and it had simply started rolling. It was a miracle they were standing there, badly scared but otherwise unscathed. "How did you get out?" I asked them.

Reynold answered, "We just got out," and that was all the light he could shed on the situation. But judging from the incline, how swiftly the wagon must have picked up momentum, how small the boys were, and how big the car door was, the only answer that came to me was that it was an angel of the Lord—not unlike the one who had rescued my Uncle Charlie when he was Reynold's age.

I called the police to report what had happened, and when they arrived, I was still comforting the boys. The officer eyed all three of us with mock severity—he was joking and may have also wanted to teach the boys a little lesson—and then asked sternly: "All right, which one of you was driving?" And he looked from one boy to the other.

Both boys were wide-eyed in fear, but Ronald, at a little over two years, was the first to speak. "Him do!" he exclaimed, pointing at his older brother, who started to cry again.

I never did scold them, but spent a lot of time giving thanks.

The building was completed on schedule, and we again brought it in well under budget, mainly because more than ten thousand hours of labor were donated. Now we could handle the 50 percent increase in attendance we were experiencing; the only trouble was, it began to look like it was going to increase that much again, in another year or two.

That Centennial year, 1967, was a celebration time for every city in the country, and every citizen who ever got a bit misty-eyed at the sight of the new national flag with the red maple leaf on white. I was president of the city's ministerial association that year, and I prayed over many buildings and pronounced many invocations and benedictions, and was so involved with civic projects, that at the close of the year, the mayor presented me with a certificate of life-time honorary citizenship.

The event that seemed the high water mark for the year took place on the morning of Pentecost Sunday. We ministers had arranged to have a combined service at the main intersection of downtown Sudbury. Traffic was blocked off, a platform was built, and people of all denominations, including the Roman Catholics, bore torches down through the streets in a great parade of Christian unity. This was the first time to my knowledge that Protestants and Catholics had joined together in a religious observance of this nature in Sudbury. The torches symbolized the tongues of fire on the Day of Pentecost, but to me what the morning symbolized was that God was indeed pouring out His Spirit upon *all* flesh, that *all* who loved Jesus Christ truly were one in Him, regardless of their denominational differences. I had been asked to speak that morning and that was the vision I shared. It was going to happen in Canada; in fact, as we bore witness, it had already begun.

In the summer of '68, we got some very bad news. We had known it was going to come, but until it actually did, we had conveniently put it out of our minds. The transition to all-color programing had been completed in the States, and Canadian stations were now scrambling to follow suit; any station which still had even a few hours of black-and-white programing was losing viewers to those who had made the shift. Therefore, Channel 9 in Toronto informed us that unless we went to color ourselves, they were going to have to drop us in September.

Here we were in Sudbury, which had only black-and-white equipment, the least expensive but still adequate color facilities being in Kitchener, six hours away. We had no choice: we began producing the show in Kitchener. We had to do it on Saturdays because our music was provided largely by Christian college students from Laurentian University, so we would leave Saturday at three in the morning, tape four or five shows when we got there, and return late in the evening of the same day. It was hard, but God blessed it mightily, and the syndication continued to expand—Calgary, Regina, and St. John were also now carrying "Crossroads."

That fall, Norma-Jean and I took our first tour group abroad—to Moscow and Egypt and the Holy Land. There were seventeen of us, most of them from our church, and we had myriad impressions and experiences which I'm sure have been shared by countless Christians who have toured these places.

A few things stand out in my memory like prized snapshots in a tour album. Preaching in the Moscow Baptist Church to a packed congregation, and then having fellowship with the Russians afterwards. We couldn't speak their language, nor they ours, but they were in tears as they hugged us and kissed us good-by. Walking through Red Square in the wee hours of the morning, a dusting of snow on the ground and Lenin's illuminated tomb looming eerily, with a few Russian people still filing through as if on pilgrimage, and the silhouette of the Kremlin hovering over everything. I realized then that the perennial depression we saw in all the faces we looked at was born of fear. And in Egypt, preaching in a church which my father had preached in, and having as my interpreter the man who was my father's favorite interpreter, about whom dad had warned me that he would get carried away and ad lib. This he did. It wouldn't surprise me if between us, we preached the best sermon I have ever given.

On the plane trip home, as we were flying over Canada, the weather was uncommonly clear, and the pilot pointed out landmarks below. As I craned to see them, my heart swelled with gratitude for my country. The sweep of it, the grandeur and majesty, the variety, were beyond description. I felt the Lord saying that He would one day use me to a far greater degree than heretofore, to reach the whole country and to help unite His people as they had never been united before. I had no idea how or when this would happen or what exactly was in store, but I didn't have to know. All I had to do was be obedient and take the next step, whenever He revealed it.

The next step became apparent as we descended. Deep inside, I felt that old stirring again, and I knew we would soon be moving.

CHAPTER 12

Sonny and Gord and
the Way Out Inn

Previously, when I had felt the stirring which presaged a move, I received a call and *then* resigned my pastorate. Now God seemed to be requiring me to resign *before* I was given any indication of what might be the next step. Through the years the Lord had been training me in obedience, to trust Him more and more implicitly, regardless of my feelings or the apparent facts. Now I was beginning to learn the instant, unquestioning obedience that saves lives on battlefields. We *were* going into a spiritual battlefield.

However, all I could see were the very good reasons why I should *not* resign—our new church was doing beautifully, and the TV ministry was expanding by leaps and bounds. We loved Sudbury, we finally had a parsonage big enough for us, and many other good things. I was not about to tell God that He should not move me; I was His servant, to do with as He would, when He would. But at least I had a duty to my family to act responsibly where their future was concerned, didn't I?

You are responsible to me, I seemed to hear the Lord say.

"But, Lord, how will I provide for my family?"

Do you trust me?

"Yes, but—"

No buts. Do as I bid you. I will provide for your family.

I could have gone on "yes, butting" all afternoon, yet by His grace I was able to choose to be obedient. I submitted my resignation to the elders, who were saddened but respected my leading. Two days later, I received a call from the Bethel Church in Hamilton. Soon to be in need of a pastor, they had felt a sudden leading to contact me. They had heard nothing of my resignation.

I went down on a Sunday morning to preach for them, and in a meeting after the service, I told them that if they voted to extend me a call, they were doing a very brave thing, because they would be inheriting a TV program as well as a pastor. And I made it clear that "Crossroads" would have to receive all the attention from me that it required. Apparently, that was fine with them; the congregation voted 96 percent in favor.

So, a few days after Christmas, 1968, the David Mainse family took up residence in the city of Hamilton, at the west end of Lake Ontario, about an hour's drive from Toronto. Hamilton took a little getting used to; it was four times the size of Sudbury and more cosmopolitan. Our parsonage and the Bethel Church were on "Hamilton's Mountain," a residential area, known for being one of the nicer sections of the city.

There was no question that the people were more sophisticated. When I preached, nothing would happen. They just sat there. They seemed to like what I had to say, well enough, and they enjoyed the singing and the praise, but there was no real spark to the meetings. There was not that sense of expectancy, that feeling that God was going to do something wonderful, right around the corner. And He didn't. No one was getting saved, no one was being healed, no one was experiencing repentance or the reconciliation of long-broken relationships—none of the things were happening that one associates with a church that is on fire for the Lord.

After four months of this, I began to wonder if we had moved out of the Lord's will. There was only one way I knew to find out: fasting and prayer. For several days I fasted and prayed, and called on others in the church who felt so led to join me. "Lord," I prayed alone in my office, "the Sudbury church was really going places for you; every day was a new adventure. Your people were really on the march up there! And this church, compared to Glad Tidings—"

But that is why I brought you here.

"But what should I do? I've done just about everything I can think of."

Except fast and pray and wait on me.

"Well, I'm doing that now," I thought, a little petulantly. "I'm sorry, Father. I see that nothing I can do will amount to a hill of beans. It will have to be you who does it."

Yes.

"Tomorrow is Sunday, Lord. Do you have a word for me? Any leading at all?"

Be bold. You have been timid. And immediately, I was convicted that that was true. I had been a little awed by my surroundings and had not spoken as forcefully or as freely as I felt like speaking.

"Anything else?"

Call on the young people to lead the way. Enough of them want to see me.

The next day I waited until the evening service, since that one was made up for the most part of our committed church family. Sensing the anointing of the Lord, and trusting Him to do whatever was necessary if I were obedient, I called the young people up on the platform and had them kneel down and silently seek the Lord. Then I called on everyone else to pray too, and wait upon Him.

Nothing happened, and the silence grew self-conscious. And then came that harassing inner whisper, telling me how foolish I looked, how foolish the whole business was. But I chose not to listen, and simply whispered, "Lord, I trust you."

Suddenly, one young man was baptized in the Holy Spirit and began to speak in tongues. That was the breakthrough we had been waiting for! The Spirit descended upon us, and that night we experienced the glory of God as strong as I have ever known it. The young man who had been baptized became something of a spokesman for the young people, calling out, "You know, pastor, I heard one of the men in this church say that things haven't been the way they used to be years ago when Brother Mallory was here. He said we had a revival back then." He turned to the other young people and declared, "I don't know about the rest of you, but as far as I'm concerned, the greatest revival that ever happened is now on!"

"*Hallelujah!*" I cried, and started preaching revival and never quit. The army of God was on the march, and our young people were in the vanguard. That night, as in the days to follow, so many people were baptized in the Holy Spirit that our church secretary, a conscientious record-keeper, gave up keeping track after the count reached 120. The atmosphere of our church was electrified, and now at services people began to experience healings, and the young people were bringing their friends in to meet the Lord.

When the Holy Spirit falls on a church, He usually falls on all age groups, and our youngest were not to be left out. At the time of our revival, we had a visiting minister staying with us, Rev. R.E. Sternall. One of the great preachers of his day, he was now eighty-six years old. He would stay with us periodically for a week or so, and he always felt at home. We, in turn, were delighted to have him, for he ministered greatly to all of us.

One Wednesday afternoon, I came home for dinner around five, and as I came in the house, I heard praying coming from our recreation room. Since no one was upstairs, I went down to see what was going on, and there were Norma-Jean and Ellen and Elaine and Reynold, and Graham Avery, the son of Hamilton's deputy clerk. All of them were on their knees, as was Brother Sternall, praising God and seeking Him with their hands raised. No sooner had I entered the room than the four children began to speak in tongues, as the Spirit gave them utterance. I was so grateful to God for allowing me to be present when it happened, and for answering my prayers that He baptize them before they became teenagers, for they would need the enabling power of His indwelling Spirit to cope with the world they were entering.

Of the three children, Reynold benefited the most dramatically. He had had a severe stammering problem that had been with him ever since he had been able to speak, and which I attributed to the difficulties and illnesses surrounding his birth. As a result, school was a place of dread for him, and in bitterness and rebellion, he had fought the system. He was eight at the time and only able to carry two units a year, spending as much time out in the hall being disciplined as he did in the classroom. His teachers knew his emotional upset had stemmed from his speech impediment, and the child psychologist and speech therapist gave him every kind of test in an attempt to pinpoint its source, but to no avail.

However, the moment that Reynold began to speak in tongues, his speech was smooth, and when he switched to worshiping the Lord in English, I was stunned! The words flowed fast and perfectly without a hesitation. Tears came to my eyes as I listened, for his rapid, clear English I knew in my heart was a form of prophecy. And sure enough, he had not been back at school two days before his teacher called us, dumbfounded. What has happened to Reynold? He seems completely different! And of course, he was. He immediately started catching up, and by the end of the school year was carrying his full load of units.

The first Sunday after this extraordinary Wednesday, Ellen, who had always had a tender spirit towards Jesus, and Elaine, who was ever alert, and noticed everything, shared in their Sunday school classes what had happened to them. As a result, a number of the girls in their classes received the baptism and tongues too! But, as I conducted the morning service upstairs, I knew nothing of this. All I could see was that Reynold was not sitting where he was supposed to be—and that meant trouble, because Reynold had a penchant for getting into as much mischief as I had when I was eight. I threw a glance over to Doris Usher, our church secretary, and nodded toward where Reynold was supposed to be sitting. She understood and slipped out of the service, and later, after church, she told me what had happened. She found Reynold in the lower auditorium. He had Graham Avery with him, and they had Richard Cunningham, a black boy in our church, stretched out on the floor behind the pulpit. I kept a bottle of oil there for anointing the sick, and as Doris arrived on the scene, Reynold was just shaking the last drops of oil over Richard. As she started to ask him what on earth he was doing, he looked up at her impatiently and said, "I need some more oil—Richard isn't getting through!" Doris smiled and joined her prayers with theirs, and Richard received the baptism in the Holy Spirit.

Revival exploded in the children's church after that. Herb Shoemaker's seven-year-old son, Roy, was one of those who received, and I will never forget coming into children's church one evening and seeing little Roy with his sleeves rolled up, going around and praying for the other children. Within a few weeks, we must have had forty-five of our children receive the baptism!

The word spread; the church grew. Norma-Jean's brother, Glen, now joined our staff as minister of youth and music, and became music director of "Crossroads." But the young people were still leading the way.

Across the street was an old gas station which the church had bought to serve the expanding need for parking space. The trouble was we were smack in the middle of an area designated by police as having the highest juvenile crime rate in the city. It didn't make sense; the young people who lived around us all came from middle-class homes. Anyone who knew Hamilton would have thought the section down at the harbor, called the North End, would have been a more likely place for such crimes. Yet the police had to know what they were talking about; they were the ones who got the complaints. And they got quite a few from our congregation. We were having the air let out of our tires and our aerials broken off, right in our parking lot.

One Sunday evening, on the way into church, Norma-Jean stopped to talk to a young girl who was sitting on the steps of the unused gas station. Every evening we had come to church, we had noticed her there, and she would be there when we came out, and now Norma-Jean decided to find out why. What she learned about the girl was heartbreaking. The girl was thirteen years old. Her parents liked to entertain, and their parties apparently got a little raunchy. At any rate, they didn't want a little girl hanging around to cramp their style. "Stay away from the house," they would tell her. "We don't care where you go, just don't come back until midnight."

"We've got to do something for these young people," Norma-Jean said with tears in her eyes. I agreed. That same morning the Hamilton *Spectator* had given front-page coverage to the juvenile crime problem in our area, and indeed some of the men in our congregation were fighting mad about what was happening to our cars across the street.

"We are *not* going to fight them," I stated emphatically from the pulpit, holding up the paper. "That would play right into Satan's hands. That's what he *wants* us to do! No, we are going to *love* them. Don't ask me how, because I don't know yet, but that's what's going to happen!"

The "how" was provided by our young married couples' group, who suggested that we renovate that old gas station across the street and turn it into a coffeehouse. And that is exactly what happened. That old building got some of the brightest paint any gas station has ever seen! The night that the Way Out Inn opened, there must have been seventy-five young people there. Speaking to the majority, who were not from our church, I said, "Okay, you've helped us get this place ready, and you know us well enough by now to know that we're leveling with you. There are no narcotics agents here, and I want to ask you a question: how many of you are on some kind of drugs?" About half of those present raised their hands, "Well, we're going to ask you not to use them here. We've got an alternative which you might find interesting, and which our young people will tell you about later. In the meantime, there's plenty of free coffee, and some pretty good music, too." And I left it up to our young people, who were supervised by some of our most mature young married couples.

The Way Out Inn was a success, so much so that we had to restrict the number of our own young people to five on any given night. This would allow enough room for all the others who wanted to come. But a certain element among the older members of our congregation thought it had become too much of a success. Many young people were getting saved, the vandalism in the parking lot had disappeared, and there were now as many worshipers under the age of thirty in our church as there were over thirty.

But that was just the problem, according to the people who were concerned. All these long-haired, hippy-looking teenagers certainly "lowered the tone of the congregation services." They always took the front pews, "to be as close to the action as possible," and a few even came not wearing shoes.

Left to itself, murmuring of this sort has a way of fanning its own flame, and pretty soon it manifested itself in a still anonymous desire to close the coffeehouse. No one would come right out and own up to wanting that—it was always "someone else overheard someone else"—but the movement was there, and I could sense it was just waiting until it felt strong enough to come out into the light.

I felt that the coffeehouse had been inspired by God, and was anointed of God, and was being used as His instrument. If so, then He would have to deal with this problem in His own way. I prayed that He would, and one night in July, He did. It happened on a night of a service of water baptism.

But first I have to tell about Gord Carter. Gord was nineteen and a natural leader, who had started coming to the Way Out Inn because of curiosity. One night we had a special event there, and I had asked an evangelist friend from Toronto, named George Leroy, to come and speak. After he had shared his message, and we were involved on a one-to-one basis with the young people, all of a sudden Gord got up and said in a loud voice, "Man, I've *had* it! That is the biggest bunch of (expletive deleted) that I have ever heard! You mean to tell me that if I come up there and get down on my knees and ask God to come into me, that something is going to happen to me?"

"Yes," George replied, smiling.

"Aw, that is too (expletive deleted) much!" Gord said, shaking his head vigorously. "Look! I'll show you!" And he came forward, got down on his knees, and snapped off a quick prayer of repentance, asking God to come into his heart. He got up, went back to his seat, and sat down. "You see?" he exclaimed. "Nothing happened."

Three minutes later, Gord stood up again, his face ashen white.

"Hey," he said, his voice breaking with emotion, "I got to tell you. When I said that before about nothing happening, I lied. I've never felt anything like this before in my life!" We took Gord to a little room and prayed with him and led him to Christ. He said he felt like bawling, and we told him to go ahead.

Gord joined our own personal family and lived with us for several months. On the night of the water baptisms, he had been one of those who had asked to be baptized. Many of the young people were also being baptized, and some of them shared their testimonies that night. But when Gord came up out of the water, his hands were in the air, and tears were mingling with the water from the tank. He asked if we could sing the song which he always wanted Norma-Jean to play, whenever she went to the piano: "He Touched Me." We all sang it with him, and I could not see a dry eye in the church. After that, we never heard another word about closing the Way Out Inn.

But probably the most moving story of all to come out of the coffeehouse ministry was that of Sonny Scholes. Sonny was a little older than Gord, and a leader in his own right. Short and wiry, he had a quick and cutting tongue, as well as a sarcastic sense of humor, which he used to great effect as a D.J. for teen dances at the local Y. Sonny had two other things: a severe alcohol problem and a desire to put an end to his meaningless and miserable life.

At this time, Howard and Nancy McIntee were the couple largely responsible for the running of the Way Out Inn. When Sonny first showed up at the coffeehouse, it was on the strength of a suggestion by a Christian nurse, who had been on duty in the emergency ward when they had pumped out Sonny's stomach from a deliberate overdose of pills. He was wretchedly unhappy, but, as Howard later said, the difference between him and most of the other empty young people who wandered in was that Sonny knew he was unhappy.

Howard and Nancy came on very low key with Sonny, eventually taking him into their home, and returning countless rebuffs and testings of their love, with Christ-like patience and compassion. And Norma-Jean and I took the same tack, always welcoming him whenever he came over. One night, he admitted later, he had slept out on our porch—too drunk to make it back down the mountain, yet sober enough to be embarrassed to ring our doorbell in that condition.

Two more suicide attempts followed, but the hound of heaven was drawing closer. Finally, on New Year's Eve, the showdown came. Howard and Nancy had invited Sonny to come with them to a watch night service, and Sonny, who hadn't had a drink in a week, had decided to go with them, even though some of his old acquaintances had invited him to a New Year's Eve bash, where there would be an endless supply of free booze. He got into the car with the McIntees, when someone called out to him, "Hey, it's New Year's Eve; how come you're not drunk?"

That did it. Sonny was out of the car in a flash, and off to the bash. He had to make it on foot, and his path took him through the park. It was bitterly cold, and as he walked, he somehow knew that if he got to the party, he was going to die. This time, there would be no eleventh-hour, stomach-pump reprieve, and in his imagination, he caught a glimpse of hell. In the lonely darkness of that park, he cried out in despair, "God, if there is a God, do something with me now." Suddenly, Sonny said later, He was there. God was with him, and Sonny reached his arms out in the darkness to Him. "Lord Jesus," he whispered, "take away this terrible blackness and break the awful chains that paralyze me inside. I'm nothing, but without you, I'll cease to even be. Give me your life, so there can be a future." And deep down inside, he felt strangely warmed.

By the time he got back to the church, it was almost midnight. There were Howard and Nancy, and he could tell by the grief on their faces that he was the cause of it. They looked up and saw him, and their faces lit up with joy through the tears. They knew, almost before he told them, what had happened to him.

Sonny was God's servant now, and in the course of finding out how God would have him serve, He took a Billy Graham writing course in Toronto, and did extremely well. He and Nancy wrote a fictionalized news documentary presentation with slides and audio tape, which dramatized the Lord's return, and called it "The Great Escape." It was shown at a number of churches in the area, and many people came to the Lord as a result. Sonny read the announcer's part himself and did a first-class job, but he was looking to find some form of writing at which he could make a living.

"Sonny," I said to him one afternoon, " 'Crossroads' is now being carried by twenty-four stations every week; maybe it's time we started to record its growth in book form. Would you be available to write the story of the TV ministry? We couldn't afford to pay you very much—"

"Would I? Pastor, the literary world has never seen a biographer like your man Sonny!" And so he began to collect background material for the story of "Crossroads." The work went slowly, but he didn't mind; he was experiencing a joy of living that he had never known before.

At the end of the summer, we took him with us out to a church rally at Kincardine, near the nuclear power plant at Douglas Point. During the course of the rally, I asked Sonny to come up on the platform and give his testimony. It was the first time he had ever spoken publicly at any length, and while he took no more than a dozen minutes or so, what he had to say had terrific impact. A number of people came forward to make the same commitment he had made the previous New Year's Eve. Driving home in the car that night, as we sang and praised the Lord, Sonny said, "This is the happiest day of my entire life."

It happened that I was leaving the next day on an extended trip that would have me out of touch for three weeks, and when I returned, my son Reynold met me in the driveway. "Dad," he said as soon as I got out of the car, "Sonny's dead." I was stunned. How had it happened? Apparently he had gotten up out of bed and walked out of Howard and Nancy's house in the middle of the night and just keeled over of a heart attack on their front lawn. Sonny had never gone back to alcohol, but its ravages finally took their toll, and it had destroyed his body, nevertheless.

But not his spirit. In sorting out his things, we came across his "Crossroads" research material—some interviews, magazine and newspaper clippings, printed material, a copy of my father's book, and a few paragraphs of prose, written in longhand on lined school paper. As I later read them, tears blurred my eyes. "In the course of a man's life lie many pitfalls, tragedies, joys and dreams. This is the story of all these, and more, for it is the biography of a vision, a family, a God, and a faith strong enough to sustain, great enough to grow. . . . I start this book with a great deal of apprehension, for it encompasses so much. It tells of a young man with an impossible vision that was to change his life. Most of all, it is to stand as proof of the reality of God and of the salvation and grace given to us through Jesus Christ."

In July, 1970, for the first time ever, our entire family took a whole month off for a vacation together. We went to the summer cottage my father and I had built on the lake just north of Kingston, and we played and swam and slept late and cooked out and went boating and hiking and singing with the guitar and sometimes we just lay in the sun and did nothing. Towards the end of that month, I had finally unwound to the point that my inner being was completely at rest, and I could begin to hear the still, small voice of the Spirit. I had not declared the vacation for that purpose, but I was tremendously encouraged by what the Lord began to reveal.

The main thing was that I began to gain an overview of our television call. I saw that it *was* a call, that we were called to national evangelism and to the work of building up the whole body of Christ. It was an overwhelming call, and the more I was able to perceive, the more inadequate I felt, almost fearful. For God seemed to be saying that what had taken place so far was only a promise of what He intended to do, as long as we continued to carry out each assignment He gave us to the best of our ability and continued to listen in our hearts and respond in obedience.

And the next step, it seemed, was to once again resign my pastorate, and this time not accept another.

CHAPTER 13

A *Christian Grey Cup Celebration*

Once again I had to battle with unbelief, and face the fact that after all God had taken me through, I still did not trust Him—not entirely without any desire to see some inkling of how it would all turn out. In the early years, we had a very small salary, but at least it came on a regular, dependable basis. Now He was not even promising that much. Donations to television ministries were, as a rule, small (though they were, quite often, all the viewer could afford at the time), and TV costs were accelerating rapidly. It was entirely possible that after our expenses were covered, we would have no salary at all. Nevertheless, God was calling me into full-time television ministry—and full-time trusting.

On the first Sunday in August, 1970, I resigned the church. The deacons were grateful for the wonderful things that had happened in their church, and although they understood God's call, they wished I could stay. I said, "Well, it's either been a very short pastorate, or a long crusade," and I left on that happy note, and was grateful to be on the other side of the pulpit, come Sunday morning. Glen stayed on with the church as music director, until he received a call to a church with a major music ministry in Edmonton, a couple of years later.

In the meantime, "Crossroads" continued to grow, and would soon have coast-to-coast coverage. We received invitations to preach and sing at various churches and the Maritime camp meeting the following summer. That winter we were given Jonah, a twelve-year-old bread van, which we fixed up with bunks and paneling and used as a family camper. We gave it the name Jonah, because all too often it was reluctant to go. For two summers, our family traveled together in Jonah, driving to the meeting sponsored by Nova Scotia, New Brunswick and Prince Edward

Island, and that trip became the highlight of our year.

Once we were at the camp, during the day I would load up Jonah with young people and take them to the nearby town of Truro, where we would witness on Main Street. My elder son, Reynold, who had just turned nine, went with us on our first foray. Somehow he got into conversation with a Moslem agricultural student, and of all things, persuaded him to come to our camp meeting. That night, the young Moslem came forward during the service and was given a Scripture by the Holy Spirit, Acts 4:12—"Neither is there salvation in any other; for there is none other name under heaven given among men, whereby we must be saved." The Moslem gave his life to the Lord, with Reynold praying for him. I was so proud that I nearly burst a button.

After that, we came down to Sunday, took the ferry across the Gulf of St. Lawrence to Newfoundland, landing at Corner Brook, and drove the five hundred miles across Newfoundland to St. John's. That drive through the strange and desolate, rocky land known as "the Barrens" is one of the most beautiful and moving auto tours in Canada. It is different from the spectacular settings at Banff and Lake Louise, which draw people from all over the world, or the awesome majesty of descending from the Rockies alongside the Fraser River to the West Coast. Crossing the Barrens is like a trip back in time—four centuries back to that time when the first Englishman landed on these shores. Except for the pavement under our wheels, the territory was virtually unchanged—and would probably remain so for the next four centuries. Our destination was Newfoundland's camp meeting at a place called Lond Pond Manuel's on Conception Bay. For the two-week meeting, I was scheduled to preach every night and twice on Sunday, and I looked forward to the warmth of their fellowship.

That camp meeting will go down in memory for my younger son Ronald too; it was there that Ellen, Elaine and Reynold decided it was time their eight-year-old brother received the baptism in the Holy Spirit. They gathered around him at the altar and began to pray, laying their hands upon him and Ronald, his arms raised and tears flowing down his face, was marvelously baptized. That night, when I went to check on the boys, to see that they were all tucked in and ready for sleep, Ronald whispered to me, "You know, dad, this being filled with the Holy Spirit thing really works! Tonight, I had to use the latrine, and you know how it's on that trail way back in the woods, and there are wolves in there and all?"

I nodded gravely, and bit my lip in the dark to keep from smiling at this wide-eyed confidence. "Well," he went on, "I had to go back there, and I couldn't find my flashlight, so I had to sort of feel my way through the bush. *And I wasn't even scared!*" I shook my head in quiet amazement.

"Dad," he said, suddenly seeming tired, "could I be water baptized too?" I nodded and gave him a hug, and on the final Sunday of the camp, I baptized him in the chilly waters of Conception Bay. There was a mass baptism service, presided over by Newfoundland's Geoffrey Shaw (who is now my executive assistant), and I will never forget that afternoon. The sun dazzled the water and shone down on some five thousand people who lined the rocky shoreline and raised their songs of glorious celebration. Those of us who were in the water joined our voices with theirs and hardly felt the cold at all. And Ronald was so happy, he became ecstatic, even though he was shivering, and we needed to wrap him in a towel as soon as he got out. Two baptisms in two days!

The faith of him and his brother and sisters has frequently been an encouragement to me, and it often surpasses my own. There was the incident with Tammy, our Chihuahua, which happened just a little before that time. Tammy was twelve years old, and the kids loved her. One by one, she had slept on the end of each of their beds when they were little, spending the longest time on the end of Reynold's bed, as if she sensed the lad's misery with his boils and then his speech impediment. In her own way, she mothered them, loving each one, which was all she could do. But her left eye had completely clouded over, and the right eye was damaged, so that she was blind. She would bump into pieces of furniture, and when she needed to go outside, she would not be able to find her way back in again, and we would have to go out and carry her in.

Ultimately, I had to make a very difficult decision, one of those when I wished someone else was the head of the family. Before leaving with Norma-Jean for a taping session at the studios in Kitchener on Saturday, the kids sent up a barrage of requests all to the tune of, "Dad, will you pray for Tammy, for God to heal her eyes?"

Trying to remember something that would help, I could only think of the time when John Wesley's horse went lame, and John Wesley had to get to a meeting. He prayed for the horse's leg, the lameness disappeared, and he was able to get there on time. So I said, "Well, Lord, you're the Creator of all mankind, and animal-kind, too," and with that we all prayed and laid hands on Tammy— which pretty well covered her up, because there were six pairs of hands and one small Chihuahua.

I had to preach in Pontiac, Michigan, Sunday, at the historic old First Methodist Church, but when we returned in the wee hours of Monday morning, we were greeted by a bounding Chihuahua, whose eyes were perfectly healed. I know my faith had nothing to do with it, because as I had driven home that night, I had dreaded the chore that I was convinced would still be awaiting me later that morning.

"Crossroads" was growing, and Satan was not happy about it. In the fall of '71, he decided to attempt to permanently derail us with a massive frontal assault. And that is a fairly literal expression. I was away preaching at Dundas, Ontario, one evening, when a deranged man grabbed two hostages at gunpoint and sealed himself into my office at "Crossroads." He had two rifles, and enough ammunition to hold off a small army for a week. He had enough food to last him that long as well, and he had a list of fancied grievances with the government that he wanted righted, as well as one or two with me personally. He also had a radio, to keep track of developments.

All of this I was blissfully unaware of, as I began to preach that night. In fact, when I noticed a policeman arrive at the back of the church, I didn't think anything of it, until word was brought to me that he wanted to speak to me outside for a moment. I slipped out, expecting to be right back, but when the officer explained the situation back at our offices, I agreed to go with him immediately. Neither of the hostages had been hurt, and they had the building well isolated and surrounded. But the man had barricaded the windows so that the police were unable to get tear gas into the room, and they were somewhat stymied.

When we arrived at the "Crossroads" offices, the situation was pretty much as it had been described. The police had established checkpoints at all the entrances to the building, allowing no reporters or other civilian personnel to pass through. There were constables with tear gas grenades, a medical team standing by, a sergeant with a bull horn, and three very grim and determined-looking men in what I assumed to be an assault team.

Norma-Jean was taken home by her brother Glen, and told to remain there until the crisis was over, but she could not bear to be there if I was in danger and, therefore, she soon returned. In the meantime, I had made my way up to the second-floor corridor where our suite of offices was. Three officers were waiting there with their pistols drawn, watching the door to my office. One of the hostages had somehow managed to escape, and informed the police that the other hostage was a real estate salesman named Frank from the office downstairs. I knew Frank; he was a very capable fellow and astonishingly fit for his seventy years, riding his bike to work every day. If somebody had to be there, Frank would be better off than most. I said a prayer for him and for the police officers, and myself as well. Suddenly one of the officers sprinted down the corridor, and as he passed the door to my office, he gave it a terrific kick and sprung it part-way open. At that instant, Frank yelled out, "I got the rifle, I got the rifle! C'mon!" There were two explosions, and a cry of pain from Frank, and I knew he didn't have the rifle any more. Those two shots motivated the second policeman to hurtle through the partly opened door with his partner close behind him. The rifle rang out again, and the first policeman clutched his chest and was spun to the ground, calling out, "I'm hit!" His partner, now starting through the doorway, found himself staring down the barrel of the rifle and dived back out for cover.

In that instant my heart was hit with a surge of adrenalin and I found myself propelled through that door. I went in low, like I was going for a hip tackle in football. I felt two bullets burning through the air on either side of my head. With strength that was not my own, I grabbed the man and the rifle and threw the rifle clattering across the room in one direction and the man in the opposite direction. The other policeman was right behind me and had the handcuffs on him in no time.

Frank was hit twice in the leg and already had his belt off, applying a tourniquet. The wounded officer was still alive; miraculously the bullet had only glanced off his breastbone! As I bent over him to see the extent of the damage, I suddenly started to shake all over as the reaction to what had just happened caught up with me.

The last I heard the man was still in Penetang, in the hospital for the criminally insane. But we have forgiven one another, and he has invited Jesus into his heart and knows the peace which passes all understanding. Whether the Lord arranges his eventual release or not, I know he has gained the release of the Spirit.

The year 1972 marked another passage. Roy L. Mainse went home to be with the Lord he had loved and served so faithfully all of his life. In 1960, after forty years in the ministry, he had asked to be retired from his last post as minister of the Wesley Chapel in Toronto. Dad had preached for me on several occasions, and I for him, and as often as I had the chance I would stop by the home that he and Elva moved into in Agincourt, one of Toronto's suburbs. We would share the things of God together and have a time of prayer, and it was more as if we were brothers in Christ than father and son. At such times, the presence of God's Holy Spirit filled the house, and tears of joy would flow.

My father had a gift for poetry, and after he had gone to be with Jesus, I enjoyed reading some of his poems, and wondering about the tender, sensitive spirit he had never let anyone get to know. After he died, I discovered this brief paragraph at the end of a testimony he had written during retirement.

"During September, 1958, I assisted in the marriage of my son, David, to Norma-Jean Rutledge of Galt, Ontario. David began preaching while still in his teens, and I have had him speak for me several times. I'm proud to have a son following in my footsteps."

For a long time, I just sat there, a lump growing in my throat. And then I thanked God for the reconciliation He had worked in our relationship, and that the bridge had been our love of His Son, Jesus.

The following is my favorite of dad's poems:

When as a child, I laughed and wept,
Time crept;
When as a youth, I dreamed and talked,
Time walked;
When I became a full-grown man,
Time ran;
When older still I daily grew,
Time flew;
Soon I shall find in traveling on,
Time gone.

In the summer of 1972, for the first (and only) time, "Crossroads" briefly climbed into the black. Customarily, donations seem to run about thirty to forty days behind our bills, which keeps us in a very needy place, very much in prayer and trusting. God has always provided, but we can never take that—or Him—for granted.

Yet here we were in the black, and I was miserable. I felt we were not reaching out like we should be. God was stirring me to do something else, but I couldn't quite get a handle on it. And then, in a suggestion made by Tom Herndon, who owned and operated a restaurant in Hamilton, it came clear. Every December, he said, the whole country goes wild for one weekend, to celebrate the Grey Cup game, which decides the championship of the Canadian Football League. Usually it's in Toronto or Ottawa, and when the western team arrives in town, so do a lot of its most avid supporters, who start celebrating Friday night, and by game time, Sunday afternoon, they are lucky if they can still find the stadium.

"Don't you think it's about time," Tom said, "that we Christians stand up for Jesus that weekend?" And it was about time. I decided that we would have a Grey Cup Christian Celebration that same weekend. It occurred to me that we could videotape it, edit it into a one-hour prime-time special, and release it across the country as soon after the Grey Cup as possible. That was the concept, and it was tremendously exciting as we initially talked about it. But later, when I sat down and took a hard look at what it would cost to buy the hour's worth of prime time on an evening, the week after the Grey Cup game, in all the major viewing areas of the country, to say nothing of the cost of videotaping six hours worth of material (we were thinking of a matinee Saturday afternoon and an evening performance that night), the figures added up to more than $75,000, and I stopped figuring.

In our national monthly newspaper, *Direction,* we told our friends what we were planning, and urged them to organize house parties and use our Grey Cup Christian Celebration as a witnessing tool. For speakers, we lined up Colonel Jim Irwin, who had just returned from the moon, Art Linkletter, Dale Evans, and of course, every Christian football player we could find in the CFL. We had to do some looking: at that time we could come up with exactly five, whereas today there are some 160 who are ready to stand up and testify for Christ. For our facility, we would use the gymnasium at McMaster, the largest enclosed area in Hamilton, which would seat 3,500. My co-chairman was to be Pastor Jim Stahl, who had played the trumpet on the street with David Wilkerson, as the latter tells in *The Cross and the Switchblade.*

And a seeming coincidence played a hand. As the football season progressed, our hometown team, the Hamilton Tiger-Cats played better ball than it had in years, and began to look like it might take the eastern division title. The city enlarged its stadium, and when the Tiger-Cats did wind up the season on top, facing the Saskatchewan Rough Riders, the Grey Cup game was awarded to Hamilton. It was all going to happen right in our own back yard!

And so it did. Thousands of western fans descended on Hamilton, and the city became the site of a gigantic house party. But the Lord was readying His celebration too. All over the country, Christians were organizing their own house parties for the following weekend, and those in Hamilton were making plans to attend one or both performances at the McMaster gym. When the long-awaited event finally arrived, it was a thrilling success. More than five thousand people attended. Everything went as smoothly and looked as polished as I could have ever anticipated.

But then came the problem of editing the tapes. We had to get six hours down to one, and in the aftermath of the Grey Cup itself, all the editing equipment in eastern Canada was tied up. I had to fly to Hollywood and do the editing there, getting back to Hamilton just in time to release the duplicate copies by courier. The press gave us a big play, of course, especially since the week after Grey Cup didn't have that much news in it to write about, and one estimate put our viewing audience at ten million—just about half the entire country. It was that high, because most of the stations replayed it between Christmas and New Year's—for free.

Best of all, we heard that hundreds upon hundreds of people got saved that night. Contributions to cover expenses came in steadily, over and above our regular "Crossroads" donations, and in less than a year our costs were totally liquidated. The cumulative impact was immeasurable. It changed a lot of people's thinking about the relevance and impact of national Christian television, and folks are still talking about it seven years later.

Our next major move came in the summer of 1973. For ten years, I had been keeping records on juvenile crime, and growing increasingly concerned about the need to reach our young people. In Hamilton, according to a police sergeant who was a friend of mine, the age of the average lawbreaker was *twelve*, where it had once been thirty-six, prior to World War II.

What had happened? I came to the conclusion that a lot of it had to do with the breakdown of the family, and the violence of television which was becoming the major influence in young people's free time. Every afternoon and evening on television, people were getting shot and killed, cars stolen and crashed, and women raped. So I began to pray, and we decided to light a candle, rather than curse the darkness. We started to put some ideas together for a top-quality, live-action children's show, which would compete nose to nose in the Saturday morning cartoon arena.

About this time, Norma-Jean's brother, Glen, had a deeply troubling experience. He was still out in Edmonton, and doing very well, when a local undertaker asked him if he would assist at a funeral service. Glen said he would be glad to, but when he arrived a little early at the funeral home, there was only a little coffin on display, less than half the normal size. Glen had asked what had happened. In the coffin was a twelve-year-old boy named Timmy, whose parents had gotten divorced and who had been sent to live with an aunt. He had grown increasingly despondent, until finally one day he had hanged himself—the youngest suicide in the history of Edmonton at that time. The divorced mother and father were shattered by this, and as Glen drove them to the cemetery, there was very little comfort he could give them, beyond trying to direct them to Jesus.

Glen was shaken by the experience. Over and over he asked himself, how did we miss Timmy? With all the churches in Edmonton, and all the Sunday schools, how did we miss Timmy? And how many other Timmys were there all across the country? Not long after that, the Lord moved on Glen's heart to rejoin "Crossroads," and he became part of our search to find the optimum video outreach to children Timmy's age and younger.

Ruby Peckford was another person who was instrumental in our arriving at the format, and what we eventually decided on was a live show, featuring eight boys and girls of different ethnic backgrounds in the eight-to-ten age group. This show had them interacting on a recreation-room type set with Ruby teaching them crafts and games and Glen teaching them songs and being a father figure. The action would be interspersed with animated cartoons, and careful editing would ensure that the pace would be lively and upbeat. Spiritually, the approach would be pre-evangelism, rather than evangelism. Jesus would be featured in the stories and songs, and Christian actions would be stressed, but it would be a more indirect presentation than a child might find in Sunday school.

The name we finally came up with was "Circle Square." In any community, the town square was the place where significant things traditionally happened, and the four sides of the square symbolized the four areas of emotional development—social, mental, physical and spiritual. The circle which enclosed the square symbolized the love of Christ, within which all our endeavors should take place.

Once again, we had to do battle in the faith department. The reason that no well-to-do church or denomination or established evangelistic ministry had ever attempted to do anything in the way of TV programing for children, was that it was impossible to raise funds in conventional ways. When adults write in to a Christian television program, they usually enclose a check.

When children write in to a TV program, and thousands of them do, it would never occur to them to send money. When an adult writes in to a program, his name often goes on a mailing list and thereafter he receives a monthly appeal letter asking for money, forever and ever, amen. (We still do not do this, and only in an emergency have we ever sent out an appeal letter, restricted to those who have previously helped us with gifts of ten dollars or more.) To ever put a child's name on such a list would be grossly wrong, and would rightly alienate the child's parents. In short, there was no way to raise the funds necessary to do a first-class children's program, unless one did so through an already existing television outreach such as "Crossroads." That is what we did, and so far, it has worked out well. We also decided to leave openings for four minutes of commercials, to make the package attractive to commercial stations.

The response to "Circle Square" was overwhelming. Eight stations offered to pay *us* for the privilege of using it, instead of the other way around! But we had decided to release it for free, in order to get as wide a coverage as possible. It went everywhere, into the States, and even down to Bermuda. After it had been on for two months, the Board of Broadcast Measurement took a survey in the Kitchener-Waterloo metro area and found that at 10 A.M. on Saturday morning, 51 percent of all the sets were tuned to "Circle Square." That meant it was ahead of all eleven other channels combined! And that was prime time for pre-teen viewing;

"Circle Square" was up against "Road Runner" and "Sesame Street" and the slickest mod cartooning Hollywood could devise!

Down in Bermuda, Ross Bailey, an old friend from the days when we had served together on the general council of the Evangelical Fellowship of Canada, and who had worked with me to form the Canadian Association of Christian Broadcasters, was pastor of the First Methodist Church. Ross had been the one to open the door for "Circle Square" in Bermuda, and now he urged us to send the "Circle Square" team down. "Everyone loves the show!" he exclaimed. "Half the island watches it on Saturday mornings. Now is the time to come down and pull in the net. I guarantee you thousands of children for an open air rally."

So, through the generosity of American Airlines, and the cooperation of the Bermuda government, particularly the public relations director, Leo Mills, who is a beautiful Christian, God worked it out. The rally was scheduled for the last Friday in September, and would take place in the show ring of the botanical gardens. A more attractive outdoor setting would be hard to imagine! The only trouble was, a hurricane had swept the island just two days before, and torrential rains were still in progress when Glen and the team landed. They started to pray, and they kept praying all the next day. And the rain kept coming. Finally, at about four o'clock, two hours before the rally was scheduled to start, the rain began to let up, and it had stopped completely by six.

In spite of the threatening weather, three thousand children came, and Leo estimated it would have been double that number had the skies been clear and the preceding rains less severe. Even so, that was a pretty good turnout for an island whose total population did not exceed sixty thousand men, women and children. Ten minutes after the rally got underway, the sky cleared and a perfect rainbow arched across the sky behind them, making a breathtaking backdrop for the television cameras. They had a wonderful time in Bermuda! The press coverage was extensive and so positive that it enabled them to go into schools. The government has invited them back, and they're looking forward to going next year.

And so things continued to grow and expand. But by the summer of 1976, although "Crossroads" was now being carried by more than a hundred and fifty master and satellite stations in Canada, I was once again growing dissatisfied and agitated. By now, I knew that kind of restlessness signaled that another major step was imminent. What it was, I did not know. At this time, Norma-Jean's brother, Ralph, was pastor of the Queensway Cathedral in Toronto, which had a television ministry of its own. Ralph and I had remained close, ever since our traveling days in Bible college, and now, with both our wives and children away visiting for a week in June, I asked him if he would fast and pray with me and wait on God, to see what He intended our next step to be.

We spent that week at Ralph's home, doing just that. At the end of the week, the Lord gave me Psalm 19, the first two verses, and when I looked them up, they said, "The heavens declare the glory of God; and the firmament showeth His handywork. Day unto day uttereth speech, and night unto night showeth knowledge." I looked at Ralph, " 'Day unto day'; you don't suppose that means daily television?" I said, and as soon as the words were spoken, we both knew it meant exactly that.

But I wanted to be sure, and asked the Lord to confirm His Word from a passage in the New Testament. And though I am not recommending it as a method of obtaining guidance, I let the Bible fall open. My eye fell on the last verse of Acts 2: "And the Lord added to the church daily such as should be saved."

CHAPTER 14

100 . . . 100 . . .

Certain now that it was time for us to move into daily television, I determined to make the move as quickly and decisively as possible. It seemed to me that we should start with the station that reached the widest live audience in Canada. That would be the Global Television Network in Toronto, which, with its satellite stations, covered all of southern Ontario, from London to Ottawa, and claimed a potential viewing audience of nearly five million.

I went to see Peter Viner, Bill Stewart, and Dan McGuire at Global, and outlined what I had in mind. The show would be ninety minutes live, would feature music and guests, and as I had envisioned in Sudbury a dozen years before, there would be telephones right in the studio, so that people could call in immediately with prayer requests or confirmations of healing, or to give their lives to the Lord. Global was definitely interested in working with us, and for a moment, it looked like this was going to be almost too easy. But then the inevitable obstacle showed up, and it was obvious that this step, just like all the others, was going to be possible only through direct intervention from on high.

We had assumed we would do the program in Global's studio, making use of their production facilities for a reasonable fee. It turned out that we would have tied up their big studio for too long, and all they could rent us was a tiny facility which would not have room for more than three or four people on camera, let alone the live studio audience, groups of singers, and telephone counselors that I had in mind. They suggested that perhaps we could videotape our music in the large studio once a week, and use canned audience response, but I knew the show would lose all its immediacy. There was only one solution: we would have to find a building large enough to hold a production studio which we would have to build from scratch.

Once again, I felt waves of doubt rolling over me. Like so many Canadians, I had become brainwashed by America's longstanding indifference to her neighbor on the northern side of the longest undefended border in the world. "Canada? That's where the cold air comes from—and hockey players—and, um—Mounties in scarlet tunics." And that seemed to be the sum total of American thought concerning Canada. Over the years that feeling had produced a national inferiority complex among Canadians, expressed in our saying, "When a mouse and an elephant sleep side by side, the mouse had better sleep lightly." That was particularly true, I felt, in the area of modern communications technology. I had been a guest on both the "700 Club" and "PTL Club," and knew their excellence firsthand. I also knew that when we finally put our own show together, it should have the same high level of quality and competence.

"Lord," I prayed one afternoon, "I'm not going to bury the talent you've given me, but sometimes I find myself tempted to think of you as a hard master."

I will not call you to any task for which I will not also make available the necessary grace.

"But, Lord, 'Crossroads' doesn't have any money at all! You know that whatever comes in goes right into renting facilities and buying air time. All we own are a few typewriters and paper clips! It will cost a million dollars just to equip a studio, providing we can find a building!"

Believe that I know your needs and have begun to meet them before you are aware of them. Pray. Listen. And believe.

"But, Lord— Yes, Lord."

And so I continued to search. I was looking for a site as close as possible either to Global's station, or to the CN Tower, the highest free-standing structure in the world, from which our signal would be sent, because the per-foot cost of a Bell Telephone line is enormous. I looked at one old warehouse after another, and each seemed more dismal than the one before—uninsulated, un-air-conditioned, un-wired, un-weathertight, unsafe, unsuitable, and un-cheap. After a depressing two weeks, the closest I had come was a decrepit old movie production studio which would cost us a million dollars just to get into, let alone to begin to equip it. I was utterly miserable.

I begged God for direction and guidance in my search, but such was my interior anguish, all I seemed to hear was the figure "100." All through the month of September, this figure kept coming into my mind; indeed, at night it almost seemed to flash on and off like a neon sign—100, 100— And typically, instead of being grateful for this much, I grew impatient.

In my desperation, I Bible-dipped. Both times, my eyes fell on Scriptures having to do with "one hundredfold," which made me more frustrated than ever. But as I prayed over these Scriptures and the hundredfold promises in the Bible, I began to see that in these end times, God was calling on all Christians to make a 100 per cent commitment of their lives. He wants them to be living in Him 100 per cent, and if they will, He intends to bless them a hundredfold. It was a strong message, and I began to see that this was to be the watchword for our daily television program—when and if it ever came to pass. "The secret of 100 per cent living"—not a bad motto. And with that, I thanked the Lord, and put the figure 100 out of mind.

Up to this point, I had not widely shared my vision for moving into daily television. Over the years, I had seen and heard too many people get too excited about dreams and concepts before they had a chance to come into fruition. These dreams would take off like verbal skyrockets, and all too often they would come crashing back to earth. But now I began to realize the only way the vision was going to get off the ground at all was with a massive, concerted prayer effort.

I began to share, first with our prayer meeting in Hamilton, as these good friends had proven themselves mighty prayer warriors on more than one occasion. And then I shared at churches or to friends, as the Spirit led, each time asking for continuing prayer for God's perfect will to be done. Finally, in October, I felt it was time to involve our "Crossroads" viewers, asking them to join us in prayer.

This concerted effort made the difference. I could feel those prayers and their support. I began to believe we were going to be involved in daily television soon. I was no longer uptight about the location. God would reveal it in His time. In the meantime, I decided to make a trip to the States, specifically to see Pat Robertson and Jim Bakker. To my knowledge, neither of those men had any plans to bring their programs into Canada, but I had to make absolutely certain of that. Nothing would be more foolish, not to say wasteful of God's money, than to try to duplicate what they were already doing.

So if either of them *was* planning to come into Canada, then instead of starting a program myself, I intended to offer my services to help them in any way I could, opening doors for them, or acting as one of their Canadian representatives, whatever they wanted. I went to Portsmouth, Virginia, and talked briefly with Pat and extensively with his network program director. They assured me that they were not going to come into Canada, especially in the wake of recent legislation requiring of Canadian television stations that at least 60 per cent of their programming be of Canadian origin.

Jim Bakker said the same thing. Inviting me to be a guest on "PTL Club," he assured me he would not come into Canada, and he would do everything in his power to help us get started. Armed with these assurances, I knew more clearly than ever that we would soon be moving into daily television. Now it was only a matter of time —and a building.

Not long after my return to Canada, I got a call from a real estate agent I had never met before, named Paul Craig. He worked for a company founded by a Christian friend named Larry Snelgrove, and he said, "Mr. Mainse, I hear through the grapevine that you're looking for a building suitable for television production. I have a building I would like you to look at." Well, one more warehouse, I thought, as I made arrangements to meet him at the building on the morning of the second Tuesday in December.

The building was on Huntley Street, directly across the Mount Pleasant Road underpass from the Confederation Life building; it belonged to Confederation Life. Despite these explicit directions, I must have driven around the block three times, before it finally dawned on me that the very large, very attractive brick building with the man standing in front of the main door was the one, and that the man was Paul Craig. I just shook my head; it was much too elegant for our use. The real estate alone had to be worth a couple of million dollars, but Paul had been kind enough to call and come down, and here I had kept him waiting, while I had driven around and around. The least I could do was be gracious enough to let him show me through the place.

Inside, we met Jim Montgomery of Confederation Life, who, I was informed, would be the man responsible for making any leasing arrangements. As these two men showed me around, I marveled at how solidly the building was constructed. It had been built in 1954, and in those days, banks and insurance companies liked to build buildings that would last a couple of hundred years. This was certainly one of them. The walls were so thick I imagined that it would withstand an atomic attack. Confederation Life had built it as a recreation centre for their employees, a place where they could have a nice cafeteria lunch and which they could use on their lunch hour or after work, for every conceivable indoor sport, from badminton to basketball. There was an elaborate exercise gym, an indoor golf driving range and a darkroom for photography buffs. There was even an accoustically-insulated, fifty-foot rifle range!

And everything was first-class, the very best that money could buy. The kitchen was practically wall-to-wall stainless steel. There were *two* enormous air-conditioning units and four heating systems that climate-controlled the entire building, *and* an air filtration unit that washed the dust out of the air. The ceilings were ten feet high, the way they used to make buildings before they became so concerned about space economy and cost efficiency. There were tall windows everywhere to let in the maximum amount of sunlight. On a clear day, the cafeteria would be more like a solarium or sun room than a place to eat. And the main gymnasium/auditorium was breathtaking—the ceiling must have been thirty feet high!

The building was certainly impressive, I admitted, as I thanked Paul and Jim for showing me around, and it would more than suit our foreseeable requirements. But unfortunately, the rental was also impressive—as obviously it had to be, since the building was insured for $4.1 million and was located on property worth at least two million dollars. I just did not see where we would ever get that kind of funding. I thanked them and left, to join Glen Rutledge and Bruce Allen, our film-maker, for lunch.

I was to meet them at a fried-chicken restaurant, and I assumed they had meant the one in the heart of the downtown area. I did not know there was another one, much nearer, where they were waiting. As I waited for them at the wrong restaurant, I began to walk up and down the sidewalk, past one pornography shop and massage parlor after another, and my spirit became so grieved for Toronto and our country, that I began to weep. I couldn't stop, and became embarrassed about what passers-by must think. But the tears kept flowing. After a while, it became apparent that we somehow missed connections, and I started walking on up Yonge Street, grieving every step of the way.

When I reached Bloor, and stood at what was called the crossroads of the country, I decided to stop in and see Earl McNutt, who had taken the pulpit of the Stone Church, which my friend Albert Vaters used to pastor, before he moved to the West Coast. Earl was in, and I asked him how it was going.

"David, frankly I'm discouraged. Here we are, almost in the shadow of St. Jamestown," he said, referring to a forest of high-rise apartments crowded into a few city blocks, and holding some fifty thousand people in the densest population concentration in Canada. "And to get the good news of Jesus Christ in there is like beating your head against a brick wall. They have every kind of shop you can think of on their ground floors—but not a single church. The churches have moved to the suburbs. There's no way to go door to door."

I chuckled. "Not even the Jehovah's Witnesses can get in there!"

But as he had been speaking, I knew there was a way. "Earl, would you do me a favor? Come and look at a building I've just been shown. It's only a few blocks from here." He agreed, and we got the key from Jim Montgomery. Looking out the windows of the building, we had to crane our necks to see the top of the high-rises next to us. "You know," I mused, "just one of those buildings holds more people than some of the villages where I used to pastor. And those villages would have four or five churches." I looked up higher, at the roofs. "But each of those buildings has a TV antenna and each apartment has a TV set." As we left, for some reason, I glanced back at the front door, and the street number in stainless steel numerals alongside it was 100.

That afternoon, as I headed for Hamilton, the sun broke out, and it was a glorious late afternoon, with the pale December sunlight casting a soft golden haze over the entire city. I drove south on Jarvis Street, heading for the lake, and the ramp that would put me up onto the Gardner Expressway, heading west. Driving up the ramp, I noticed that the expressway on either side above perfectly framed the CN Tower which was aglow in the light of the setting sun. In that instant, *I knew* the building was ours! God assured me that He was going to open the doors and make the impossible come to pass! And something else: I saw the significance then of the building's address—*100* Huntley Street.

So *that* was what He had meant! He had known our needs since before the foundation of the world! Confederation Life had thought they were building a recreation centre, but God knew they were building a television studio. Hallelujah!

The pieces fell into place quickly after that. Two nights later, there was a meeting in Toronto of Candian evangelists, and I invited a few of these men to join me in a victory march around the recreation centre, claiming it for Jesus Christ and the glory of God. Don Osborne, a tall fellow from Vancouver, and Reyn Rutledge came with me and we tramped through the snow around the building, grateful it was a dark night. Don, who is on our staff now, still kids me that he claimed more territory than I did, because his shoes were size fourteen.

We arranged with Jim Montgomery to lease the building for twenty years, with an option to extend the lease for an additional five years, though we fully expected the Lord to return long before the year 2002. We were granted an extremely reasonable final rental figure, and the papers were drawn up and signed in an incredible six weeks, which in itself was a miracle.

But now we had passed the point of no return. The second major miracle occurred when we met with representatives from RCA, to talk about our equipment needs. I was surprised at how important they seemed to think we were—until I realized that the Holy Spirit had been doing a good deal of preparatory work in their hearts. In any event, to meet with us they sent up some of their top people from their New Jersey headquarters—their general sales and credit managers for all countries outside of the United States, also their sales and credit managers for Canada, and their Toronto sales representative. On our side of the table were John Riegert, a personal friend and advisor who was secretary-treasurer of the Canadian Bankers Association, and Howard McIntee, my right-hand man on the technical side, who was a member of our congregation in Hamilton, and had been a great help in producing "Crossroads."

We outlined our needs, and before they left the city, they said they would supply us with everything on our list, advancing credit to us for nearly a million dollars.

Moreover, they would give us six months to come up with the down payment of 25 per cent, and the remaining 75 per cent would be paid off over the next five years, at an interest rate better than we could have gotten from conventional lending institutions! Finally, they actually delivered much of the equipment before the down payment had been made. God answers prayer!

With that great need taken care of, the Lord laid it on my heart that we were to announce that the first daily broadcast of "100 Huntley Street" would take place on June 15, 1977, less than four months away. And now major miracles started occurring thick and fast. The next concerned our wiring and air conditioning, and it was one of the before-the-event variety that were such a wonderful assurance. Studio lights, cameras and control room equipment took a tremendous amount of electricity, and we had two engineers come in to assess our needs. These men had designed two other large television studios in the city, and when they were finished checking everything, they shook their heads in disbelief.

"You know, somebody up there really likes you people!" one of them exclaimed. "First of all, there are no walls that need to be moved. It's almost as if this place were laid out to be a studio. Secondly, the electrical equipment you already have here is so much more than a recreation centre would ever need, that it will take very little to adapt it for a studio's purposes." He chuckled. "But the wildest thing of all is that air filtration plant! A control room, like a computer room, has got to be dust free; the greatest enemy of a tiny, solid-state circuit is a speck of dust. Dust can reduce the life span of your equipment by as much as two-thirds, to say nothing of being a constant aggravation. Normally, it takes highly sophisticated air cleansing equipment to protect your electronic investment. Not so here. This entire building is virtually dust free!"

The electrical adjustments were made, the control room set up, and now we needed a grid of steel pipes suspended from the ceiling of the gym to hold all our lights and speakers and microphone outlets and other electrical paraphernalia which was commonplace to technicians and totally bewildering to myself. There was nothing bewildering, however, about the two estimates we got for the job: $32,000 and $33,000. But as I prayed to see which of the companies the Lord would have us use, I got a check in my spirit. Apparently, He didn't want us to use either one. I was impatient, because now every day counted, if we were going to be on the air by June 15, but I knew I had to wait.

Two days later, a man strolled in off the street. "What's going on around here, anyway?" he asked me. "What's all that electrical equipment for?" And I told him.

"Well," he said, "you know, I build stands."

"What sort of stands?" I asked, to be polite.

"I built the reviewing stand for the Queen to stand on, when she came to Montreal. Things like that."

"What do you build them of?" I asked, suddenly interested.

"Steel pipe, why?"

"Because we just might have something you can do for us, right here." He did the job for $12,000. We had saved $20,000, because God happened to give a passer-by a desire to turn in and see what was going on at "100 Huntley Street."

Something similar to that happened when it came time for us to get our lighting board. This was a crucial and very expensive piece of equipment. It was worth $20,000 and the company we had ordered it from would not release it until they had our cheque in hand for the full amount. Needless to say, we didn't have even a tenth of that amount in our account, nor had we established a line of credit at any banks in Toronto. But if we had to wait until we raised such a large amount, we would not open in 1977 at all, let alone June.

"What do we do now, Lord?"

Send the cheque.

"Lord, you've taught me a lot about faith, but—"

Send the cheque.

"Yes, Lord."

That night, I learned later, Jack McAlister of World Literature Crusade was awakened out of a sound sleep by the Lord, who told him to send David Mainse $10,000 right away. Jack had never met me, though his father, Walter McAlister, had been the minister who had prayed for me when I was ordained into the ministry. Jack later related that he had tried to bargain with God, asking if $5,000 wouldn't be enough. But God emphasized it was to be $10,000 and so Jack called our home at seven o'clock in the morning (which was four his time) and told Norma-Jean. Within hours, two other men were similarly touched, giving $5,000 each, to make up the remainder. Not only were these the biggest gifts we had ever received, it was the first time I had ever heard of an established ministry like Jack's making such a gift to another ministry that was just starting.

Of all the miracles of that spring, the greatest by far were those God was doing in the lives of the people whom He was raising up to help us. Even if nothing else had happened, these things alone would have been ample confirmation that the work was God's and His alone.

CHAPTER 15

Walking Miracles

I wish I had room to tell the story of how every person who joined us had the direction of his or her life suddenly altered by God, to enable them to come on board. In fact, my friend and co-author, David Manuel, tells me we have enough material right now for the start of another book, so perhaps there will be another someday. We might even call it *Friends of the Family* since it would be about the "100 Huntley Street" family and our friends across Canada; in the meantime, I must beg the forgiveness of all our loyal employees whose stories I am unable to squeeze into this chapter. As of this writing, there are some one hundred twenty on our payroll, and I only have room to write about a few of them.

The fitting story to open with is that of my friend with the size-fourteen shoes. Don Osborne is in charge of what I call our "People's Division," and is responsible for establishing our telephone counseling centres across the country. At the moment there are more than one hundred phones in use throughout Canada, and approximately six hundred trained counselors standing by to man them. Don is also in charge of follow-up, which has always been a vital concern of mine, ever since my Chalk River days. It is especially important in an open-phone ministry since we are receiving nearly two thousand commitments to Christ every month, and more than fifteen thousand requests for counseling.

Don had had a burden for such a ministry, ever since he was founding director of Teen Challenge for Western Canada, and had inexplicably started to weep at the sight of a newspaper picture of some high-rise apartment buildings several years ago. He had no idea what it meant then, but the same thing happened to him again three years ago, as he was landing in Toronto for a meeting. He saw the high-rise apartment buildings near the airport, and was overcome with unexplained grieving. That was the night when I first shared with him my vision for daily Christian television, but the idea was so alien to him that he did not see himself ever getting involved in such a work. He was much in love with the beautiful mountains of British Columbia where he lived, and it would take "Holy Spirit dynamite" to ever dislodge him.

And so there finally came the night when we marched around 100 Huntley Street, and I said, "Don, I know you're supposed to be with us here. How much longer will you be in the city?"

"I'm leaving in the morning to go back to Vancouver."

"Don, I want you to fly from here down to Charlotte, North Carolina, to see PTL's operation and get an idea first-hand of what daily television is all about. We'll have a ticket waiting for you at the airport."

"Can't do it, David. I've been here three days already, my seat on the plane is booked, and the board of a church back home has asked me to be their pastor, effective immediately. I have a meeting with them as soon as I get home."

Normally, I wouldn't push, but I was so sure I had heard the Lord that I could not let it go. "All right, but promise me you'll at least pray about it before you leave." He assured me that he would.

The next morning, Don woke up two-and-a-half hours before he was due to leave, and our conversation was heavy on his mind. "Okay, Lord," he prayed, "obviously this thing is important. But you're going to have to speak to me very clearly, or otherwise I'm going home."

Don does not recommend Bible-dipping either. He is much more in favor of studying the Word carefully. But that morning, he did what he almost never does: he opened his Bible at random. It opened to 1 Samuel 20:18, 19: "Thou shalt be missed because thy seat will be empty. And when thou hast stayed three days, then thou shalt go down quickly."

He was staggered. Each phrase hit him with such impact that he wept before the Lord. He went to Charlotte (which happens to be due south of Toronto), received all manner of confirmation in his spirit, and called to say he would be joining us as soon as he could move his family.

Ian Taylor did not like TV. He would not have a television in his home, and had never heard of me or "100 Huntley Street" when his friend, Lorne Shepherd, also of Kingston, told him of the new television ministry that was forming in Toronto. But after twenty-one years as a research engineer in metallurgy with the Aluminum Company of Canada, Ian had asked the Lord for a change of employment. Within a month, he had left his job and was looking for full-time Christian employment. Lorne put him in touch with us, and he volunteered to work for no salary if we would find something for him to do.

As it happened, he had experience designing lighting for an amateur theatre and we badly needed a lighting engineer, so another piece of the puzzle went into place. Ian joined us in mid-April of 1977, just in time to pitch in to the massive, all-out effort to get air-borne by the fifteenth of June. Today, Ian is producer of the new "Crossroads" series, which has shifted its format from testimonies to teaching. It's still a weekly, half-hour show, but now it is a one-on-one discussion of subjects like the theory of evolution from the Christian point of view. One recent program on the defense system of the human body against infection drew an incredible response of five thousand letters! And since he has a real gift for technical trouble-shooting and organization, he is also in charge of maintaining our studio equipment. (I should add that we took him up on his offer to work for free only for the first month; thereafter, we could afford to pay him a salary.)

If your set is tuned to "100 Huntley Street," the first thing you'll hear over our film clip and theme song is something like, "Hello, everyone, and welcome to '100 Huntley Street'! We invite you to share the next ninety minutes with us, and with people just like you. . . . So relax, have a cup of something warm, and get to know the people who have discovered the secret of 100 per cent living."

That voice belongs to an Anglican priest named Al Reimers (who was once in the U.S. Army's counter-intelligence corps and even slept with a .45 under his pillow!). Al's path first crossed mine in Sudbury fifteen years ago, where I followed him as president of the ministerial association. Al was doing telecasts for that organization at the same time I had begun doing "Crossroads" out of Sudbury, so we got to know one another even better at the TV station.

Then Al received the baptism in the Holy Spirit, and our relationship took yet another turn. That was back in early 1965, when the charismatic renewal was just beginning to touch the liturgical denominations, and Al exercised wisdom in keeping largely silent about his experience for the first several months, until he had had a chance to grow and mature. When the time came for him to share, I invited him to come to Glad Tidings and give his testimony, and it was a great blessing.

We lost touch when Al moved away from Sudbury, but early in 1977, I got a call from him. He was doing a book on the charismatic renewal in Canada, and he wanted to come and interview me as to the role of radio and television in the renewal. It was an unusual interview, because after he finished asking his questions, I started asking mine. How soon could he join our staff? He pleaded that he was already committed to the book project and could not undertake anything further until it was finished. I asked him to at least pray about it, because he wouldn't want to miss the Lord, if He wanted him to join us now. We would give him large chunks of time in which to finish the book, and in the meantime, there were all sorts of things he could do, like announcing, and occasional co-hosting, and helping the telephone counselors by handling particularly difficult calls, like those from suicidal people. He did pray, and wound up accepting the job. And by the way, if you're interested in what the Holy Spirit has been up to in Canada, I can warmly recommend a book called *God's Country*, by a fellow named Reimers.

There's another priest on the program, but he prefers a tie to a collar, and with a mischievous twinkle in his eye, he looks more like a leprechaun. He also has a warm smile, and a sweet, bubbling spirit that goes with the twinkle, and the cumulative effect is the opposite of what one might expect from a Jesuit. No one is more surprised and delighted at what God has done in his life than Father Bob MacDougall himself. His open, buoyant personality has endeared him to millions of viewers, but it was not always thus. There was a dark side to Father Bob once, a side that took him to the pit of despair and came close to destroying his life.

Father Bob was born and raised in Halifax, Nova Scotia. His mother died when he was four, and perhaps that was where his insecurity and fears began. During the war, he was a tail-gunner with the RCAF, flying night missions over Germany, and his position, back in the tail of a Lancaster bomber where he felt cut off from the rest of the crew, seemed to symbolize his life. In the daytime, he would chase and carouse around England with the hard-drinking and wenching buddies from Australia and New Zealand he flew with, but every night when he went on a mission, he flew in terror. And it got worse, with each mission he flew. He would look out at the night sky, and see other Lancasters in his formation being shot down, and wonder if tonight would be the night. Down below, cities were in flames and in his mind's eye, he could see his own plane falling out of the sky, into those flames. And he would fall right through them into the eternal, sulfureous flames of hell. For Bob knew God was real, and he knew there was a hell.

Finally, three missions before his tour was to end, the thing Bob feared the most came upon him. His crew had been selected for a special mission that night—dropping medical supplies, radios and weapons to the Danish underground. This meant they would be flying solo and staying below 300 feet, to fly under the German radar defenses. Hugging the ground, his Lancaster worked its way into a fjord and inland up a river, flying so low that at one point they passed under a bridge. At the designated drop zone, they briefly ascended to 700 feet, just high enough for the parachutes to open, and then, mission accomplished, they dropped back down to the deck, and made their way out of Denmark.

The closer they got to the Danish coast, the more they began to relax, and as the shoreline flashed underneath them, they were all in high spirits, cracking jokes on the intercom, and shaking off the tensions of the flight. And Bob, instead of scanning the sky behind them, was celebrating the fact that in two more runs he would be going home. He never noticed the darker silhouette that had been shadowing them. Suddenly, the orange flashes of the Messerschmidt's guns burst in the night, and he felt the sickening impact of the shells slamming into the fuselage. The plane was so low, and it happened so suddenly there was no room to maneuver. The engines hit, and the plane plunged headlong into the sea.

As it hit the water, the tail section broke away from the rest of the plane, which sank like a stone. Bob was somehow thrown clear, the only one of his crew to survive. Somehow, a rubber dinghy had detached itself from the wreckage. He grabbed onto it, and it kept him afloat, until he was picked up by some Danish fishermen. Fearful of being caught if they tried to help him, they left him to wander the countryside. For several days he traveled by night until he finally grew so hungry that he went to a farmhouse to beg for food. When they denied him food, he drew his pistol and took it from them. After that, the Germans tracked him with dogs, and before long he found himself in a prison camp, where he remained for the last year of the war.

After the war, he went to university, to conquer his fear and guilt through the power of his intellect. And at the same time, while he feared God and His judgment most of all, he felt strangely drawn to Him. Bob began to study for the priesthood, specifically to become a Jesuit. It was a vigorous thirteen-year program after university and at the end of each year he hoped the next year would hold some of the joy his heart told him had to be there somewhere. Perhaps it would finally come with ordination—

But it never did. His training was in clinical psychology, and he went to Latin America, where it seemed there was more crying need than anywhere else on earth. But two years there were all he could take, for he had nothing to give but sympathy, and, more depressed than ever, he returned to Canada. Eventually he found himself in the prison ministry at Stony Mountain penitentiary in Winnipeg. Trying to help inmates with everything from Transcendental Meditation to encounter group therapy, he found none of these things really helped anyone. He began to depend on drugs to help himself—uppers to get going, downers to relax, and ultimately alcohol, to keep him thinking.

Finally, he wound up in a small, church-run psychiatric hospital in Toronto in 1973, his life in ruins. He had given up on himself, and it was there that God reached out to him. A young priest who was an out-patient in the same hospital had been to something called a charismatic prayer meeting, and had experienced something so extraordinary that it had shaken him badly. For he had suddenly seen a picture of Bob's face, and heard the words, "Lay hands on this brother, for tonight I will heal him."

He came home and told Father Bob about it, and while he was skeptical and even sarcastic, he did get down on his knees and allow the young priest to pray for him. The next thing Father Bob knew, he was flat on the floor and feeling a vast warmth all over. He was laughing and crying and felt what he could only describe as waves of love washing over him. He knew he had been reborn of the Spirit. After about twenty minutes of this, he was able to get up off the floor, and he staggered to his room, because he felt this great upwards pressure under his rib cage and feared that he was about to be sick to his stomach. What happened instead, was that a heavenly language sprang forth from his lips and went on for another fifteen minutes, while he continued to experience inner healing. He couldn't define it exactly, except that he knew he would never have to take another pill or another drink.

Father Bob's life shifted into high gear after that. Like many newly baptized charismatics, he had a tendency to leap on his horse and ride off in all directions. Finally he realized that he had to give over the total direction of his life to God, and he went on a week-long desert retreat. At the end of a week of fasting and prayer, God told him that he was to work with us. Knowing us hardly at all, he courageously came to Toronto, found us, and offered his services. That was before the brigade that became the "100 Huntley Street Irregulars" started to form, and as soon as it did, we got in touch with him. He reported for duty in February of 1977, just in time to grab a paint brush and help us get ready. So, that's the story behind that beaming face under the shock of gray hair, a story that most people would never guess to look at him. For Father Bob has really learned the secret of 100 per cent living!

Another person who never expected to be here was the executive secretary of the Newfoundland Pentecostal Education Committee, Geoffrey Shaw. A chartered accountant in England, converted at the Billy Graham Crusade in 1954, Geoffrey had gone to Kenya as a self-supporting missionary. There, he met and married Albert Vaters' sister, Pauline, and returned with her to Newfoundland. Geoffrey had been in Christian day school administration in Newfoundland for twenty years, during which time he had seen Christian schools increase in Newfoundland and Labrador, until there were fifty-three of them, with 6,500 young people enrolled, and 350 teachers, etc. When one stops to think that the total population of those provinces is only a little over half a million, that is an impressive figure!

I had known Geoffrey for many years and when it became apparent I would have to have an administrative right-hand man, Geoffrey was the one whom God laid on my heart. Unfortunately, "100 Huntley Street" was not at all on Geoffrey's heart when I broached the subject to him. The thought of his ever leaving his beloved Newfoundland was more than he could bear.

But a funny thing had happened to him just a week or so before I called. Of all his responsibilities, the one he enjoyed the most was teaching the trainee student teachers the ins and outs of Chrisitian education. Geoffrey had developed a very positive point of view—that the Christian approach had every bit as much logical validity, because it was impossible for the atheists to prove that God did *not* exist—and he delighted in imparting his enthusiasm to his new trainees. Yet suddenly, he found himself wondering, almost drearily, if he *had* to teach that same course again in the coming fall. Thus, while his response was a categorical no, when I called, it was not really as categorical as it sounded.

That weekend he had a preaching engagement in Stephenville, but when he got there, he found he couldn't pray! It was a decidedly unnerving experience. "Lord," he cried out, "can it be possible that you really *want* me to leave Newfoundland and go to work with David?" And as soon as he said the words, he knew it was true. He gave in then, and not too surprisingly, the ability to pray returned. Geoffrey came on staff as soon as he could get his affairs in order, and has been a burden-lightening blessing ever since.

It is not every day that one finds a key producer/director living as one's neighbor; perhaps it doesn't happen more than once in a century. But that is what happened with Malcolm Neal, the director of "Circle Square" and "Inside Track." In 1971, back in Hamilton, I had just gone full-time into the production of "Crossroads," and one day, shortly before we were scheduled to broadcast, the director we were then using was not able to be there. Hearing of our plight, Malcolm, who had extensive experience in secular TV as a director in Britain and Canada, offered to fill in. From that day on, he directed every "Crossroads" show, until his work on our other programs made it impossible for him to continue.

Malcolm was a talented director, projecting the calm, unflappable poise which was so vital in the control room where everything seemed to be happening at once, and errors had a way of compounding themselves with astonishing rapidity. If something started to go wrong, you could bet it would soon go *very* wrong, if somebody didn't have the situation well in hand—or at least give the impression that he had. Malcolm had the ability to quench the brush fires of panic before they could become all-out conflagrations.

But Malcolm himself had not yet tasted the Living Water that quenches the greatest thirst of all when we first met him. We had a leading to go slow with him and his wife, Kerry, and when the time seemed right, Norma-Jean gave Kerry a copy of Pat Robertson's book, *Shout it from the Housetops*. She was moved, and gave it to her husband, who was mildly interested. Here was the story of another fledgling entry into Christian television, one that he could relate to from a professional point of view. Malcolm started coming to our church. In the space of three intensive months, he came into an intimate relationship with Jesus, and the effect on his work was subtle but significant. His creativity blossomed, and while calm and collected when the chips were down, now he was looking outside of himself for his strength.

Actually, the first person to come on the "100 Huntley Street" payroll was an evangelist who had specialized in follow-up: Clyde Williamson. Again, the Holy Spirit began the work of drawing him our way long before he came. In fact, as soon as he had experienced the infilling of the Holy Spirit, he found he had such a burden for his native land that all he could do was cry out "Oh, Canada, oh, Canada," over and over.

The burden received some definition in January of 1976, as he was praying in the little Quebec chapel of his friend, Rev. Lindsay Stevenson (who is now the producer of our new French program, "Au 100 Tuple"). Both of these young men were earnestly seeking direction for their lives and both received one word: television. Ten months later, Clyde received his next clue. This time he was praying in a church in Fredericton, when he received the distinct impression that the Lord was about to move him to Toronto.

Upon returning to the little trailer in which he was traveling with his wife and two daughters, she greeted him with, "Guess what happened while you were gone? I got the funniest feeling that we were moving to Toronto—do you suppose it was the Lord?"

They arrived in Toronto on December 23, and right away looked up Ralph Rutledge, pastor of the Queensway Cathedral, whom Clyde had been close to for a long time. That same night, Ralph told him, "I think you ought to see David Mainse. He's about to pioneer a work in television."

"Is that right?" responded Clyde, marveling at how many pieces of the puzzle were fitting together all at once. The next day, Ralph took him through the facilities at 100 Huntley Street. As he was coming down the stairs at the north end of the building, he heard the Holy Spirit speak in his heart, as clearly as He had ever spoken: *Clyde, this is where I want you to work.*

Ralph was standing with several other men at the foot of the stairs, and he asked, "What do you think?"

Clyde could hardly answer. "Well," he finally managed, "I don't know about the rest of you guys, but God has just told me I am going to be working here." Three days later, he was. Today he is responsible for the area of personal follow-up, and has just initiated a forty-eight-hour call-back program, in which every individual who calls in to give their life to Christ, or to ask for prayer, receives a follow-up call. Clyde is also responsible for making sure new Christians are referred to churches in their local area. "100 Huntley Street" is interested in building up the whole body of Christ. And we do not favor any one denomination over another; if a person has a denominational preference, we will refer him to the nearest church of that denomination where he will get the spiritual nourishment he needs.

The big miracle connected with Bob McKenzie's coming to "100 Huntley Street" happened a couple of weeks *after* we had gotten the show on the air. Bob was the son of two totally deaf parents, who himself had hearing in only one ear. He was a born-again Christian, and because of his hearing problem, he was surprised when the Lord seemed to be indicating that instead of going to Bible college as he wanted to, he should major in communications. He was obedient, and he applied to Ryerson Polytechnical Institute which had one of the best communications departments in the world, figuring that if it *was* God leading him, somehow he would open the impossible door.

God did exactly that. With a great deal of hard work, Bob earned his degree—just about the time God began recruiting His Huntley Street Irregulars. Bob's training, theoretical as it was, was still more than most of ours, and we gladly welcomed him aboard. His first assignment was that of floor manager, which meant he was responsible for relaying the director's commands from the control room, cuing the cameras and the on-screen personnel and generally keeping track of everything that was happening on the set.

Bob loved the job and was good at it. His enthusiasm was contagious, and it helped us to relax, as we were all pretty uptight in the beginning. One day, a couple of weeks after we had started, we had just arrived safely at the end of another ninety minutes live, which was a little like a novice tightrope walker must feel when he finally reaches that platform at the end of the high wire. On this particular morning, however, the anointing of the Holy Spirit was so pronounced that everyone noticed it. Suddenly, one of our cameramen, Paul Pickerim, who had bent too low to yank his camera truck out of the way, gave a loud groan and doubled over, falling to the floor. There he lay, moaning and writhing in pain, clutching his lower back, where he had apparently torn or pulled something.

Bob was one of the first to get to him, and he called for someone to get a doctor. Father Bob and I were next on the scene, and we said, "Let's pray for him." As Bob McKenzie related it later, Father Bob was praying by his right ear, and since that was the one he had no hearing in, he could barely hear him. But then he began to hear him more and more clearly. He held his hand over his left ear, and his eyes widened in amazement. He started clicking his fingers of his right hand next to his ear. And then he jumped up and started shouting. "Hey! I can hear! *I can hear!*" Just then Paul got to his feet, too; they had both been healed.

We all took that as a tremendous encouragement from the Lord; it was as if he was putting His signature on the work, and saying, *Come and see what I am doing this day in Toronto.*

Jim and Marian Poynter, who had both been at Annesley College back in the days when my father was director there, are longtime friends. In fact, Jim was the young ex-soldier who had been climbing the front steps, only to have my father lock the door on him, because it was past ten o'clock. And Marian was the girl my mother had told to keep an eye on Jim, because they were not too sure of his salvation. She did, all right, and still is.

Jim is directly responsible for selecting and training the telephone counselors, and Marian is one of those counselors. She has a lovely motherly way about her, and it projects nicely through the phone, with a decidedly calming effect on some of our more distraught callers. Nor is it surprising that she should have a motherly spirit; in addition to four children of her own, and three grandchildren, she and Jim have raised thirteen foster sons, and nineteen other young people who have lived in their home at various times.

Jim loves being where the action is, and as far as he's concerned, the action is on the phones. Nothing is more thrilling to him than to answer a phone right after a strong salvation testimony by a guest or an invitation by myself, and hear a quavering voice saying, "Please, could you tell me how to accept Jesus into my heart?"

Jim varies his response to fit the mood and needs of the caller, praying silently for the Holy Spirit to show him what is needed.

One counselor who has been with us from the very beginning is Regina Schlomer. Actually, Regina had her own telephone ministry of sorts, before she ever came to 100 Huntley. She is one of those people who just simply care about others, and who would go all over Toronto, praying for people on subways, in supermarkets, in hospitals—but always as the Spirit led, and only when He led. She would lead people to Jesus, and then she would give them a call a few days later, to see how they were doing. Inevitably, they would start calling her too, until her line at home was so jammed with calls that her husband complained. Yet each time she was about to call the phone company to get a second phone, the Lord said no; He would give her a second phone.

In the meantime, God had laid such a burden on Regina's heart for Christian television that she had begun praying for a daily program, a year and a half before I did. God had even told her that one day she would pray for the entire nation of Canada on television, something which seemed so impossible to her since she was German by birth and her English was not too good. Therefore, she soon forgot about it.

When she heard we were starting a television work, she called to recommend someone else for a job, and I asked her what was she was doing herself. "Oh, I am waiting for a second phone that the Lord is going to install for me."

"Well, come on down, Regina," I chuckled. "I think I have the phone for you." And she did. Three days after we started broadcasting, I suddenly felt led while on the air to take over to Regina a pile of prayer requests we had received from all over Canada, and ask her to join me and pray for them and for all of Canada, while she was at it. As we prayed, I was surprised to see tears running down her cheeks, until she explained the prophecy which had just come true.

God seems very close to Regina whenever she is on the phone; He tells her what to say and what not to say, and even what conditions He will heal, if she will pray for them. And as has happened on more than one occasion when all thirty phones are in use, a very troubled German girl will get Regina, converse in German and hang up, then call back, and be routed through to Regina's phone again, and again hang up and call back, and again get Regina. I don't know what the odds are of getting the same person out of thirty, three times in a row, but they are high enough to bear witness to what all of the phone counselors know: the Holy Spirit routes each one of the calls to the particular counselor He has picked to handle the call.

The last person I will tell you about is production division head, Lorne Shepherd. Like Don and Geoffrey and one or two others, Lorne was one of the draftees in the "Huntley Street Irregulars." A small-town fellow by his own admission, he had a very successful career in television in Kingston, directing some of the local station's most important shows. He had worked there for twenty-four years, and had no desire to leave, except for retirement. And concerning that retirement, he and a partner had a subdivision which they were hoping to develop, if they could get the funding, and Lorne had a piece of land all picked out for his retirement home.

"Lorne," I told him, on the third occasion of my speaking to him about coming to Toronto, "I know you're God's man. I don't believe the Lord will let you settle into the comfortable future you have all mapped out for yourself." And that turned out to be a prophetic word. After that, every time Lorne opened his Bible, the words that leapt out at him had to do with getting up and going somewhere, or arising and going to Jerusalem, and the like. He held out for a long time, but in the end, he knew there was no use bucking God. But he still didn't want to move until the financing was resolved.

"Lorne," I told him one evening in our home, "God wants you *now*, not when you've bought a cow, or got a wife, or acquired a piece of land."

"All right," he capitulated, "but if we don't have financing, I could go bankrupt. And I know God did not give us that land, to see that happen to it. All I'm asking is that He give me some reassurance about the financing." He opened his Bible to Matthew 6:25, "Therefore, I say unto you, Take no thought for your life, what ye shall eat, or what ye shall drink; nor yet for your body, what ye shall put on. Is not the life more than meat and the body than raiment?"

So much for security—but Lorne still felt no sense of call to live in Toronto. His wife did, though, and so did his daughter, and one evening as the sun was going down, he noticed that Toronto was really a surprisingly beautiful city, yet still he hesitated. Finally, I gave him a deadline: October 15. By that time, we had been in operation for four months and Howard McIntee had had to carry the responsibility for shaping up production. The fifteenth came, and there was still no financing, but after much agonizing, Lorne moved anyway. The next morning his lawyer called with the news that the Bank of Montreal had just approved the financing, and given him better terms than he had ever heard of! "Behold the fowls of the air: for they sow not, neither do they reap, nor gather into barns; yet your heavenly Father feedeth them. Are ye not much better than they?" (Matt. 6:26). Are ye indeed!

The week leading up to our start on June 15 was one that none of us who lived through it will ever forget! As usual, I was into everything, helping everywhere I could (and hopefully being more of an asset than a liability). It was an exciting time—even more exciting than building a new church, because we were doing something that had never been done before in Canada. Most of us were flying blind, trusting the holy Spirit to keep us from making horrendous errors, and to guide us in what to do next. Talk about a faith-walk! We were so far out on the water that we did not dare to take our eyes off of Jesus!

It was exciting, but like wartime, it was also exhausting; it felt as if we were in a staging theatre, preparing for a major offensive, and had only seven days left to get it ready, when we needed seven weeks. And like mounting such an offensive, once all the machinery had been put in motion, it was almost impossible to stop. And so the Huntley Street Irregulars rolled on towards the fifteenth, hardly any of us believing we were actually going to make it, yet each of us obediently putting one step in front of the next anyway.

By this time we were moving automatically, most of us functioning on four hours of sleep or less for countless nights. But we *were* functioning, and that was the main thing. No sooner would one task be completed than we would wearily but cheerfully move on to the next. And as we did, we grew closer to one another than we had ever been before. It *was* a bit like combat, with everyone unusually sensitive to the needs and feelings of others. Many nights I worked so late that it was just easier to lie down on a mattress on the floor to grab a few hours of sleep, and there were others doing the same thing.

The night before the fifteenth, no one slept at all. We worked all night, and I am sure I wasn't the only one in despair over the chaotic mess our studio was in —carpeting and carpentry mess everywhere, no lights up on the grid, the phone banks not yet finished, the camera cables a hopeless rat's nest, and the studio clock whisking hours away like annoying flies. Three o'clock, four, five—"Sun's up," someone called out, but no one looked up from what they were doing—it was still dark in the studio. Six o'clock, seven, eight—still no change, except the tempo and noise of pounding and hammering and sawing increased.

I looked around and could see no discernible improvement over what it had looked like six hours before! If we had to go on at 8:30 instead of 9:30, we would not physically be able to get a signal out, it was as simple as that. And the same could be said at 9:00—the studio lights were up on the grid, but there was still no power, nor were we yet in reliable contact with our control room, which was parked just outside the studio. We'd had to borrow Gordon Emerson's mobile unit, as our own control room was not yet wired up.

Now great gobs of minutes were simply disappearing without a trace. Before I knew it, Bob was calling out, "Five minutes to air!" The studio audience was in their seats, the phones were all manned, the interview set was miraculously ready, but the music set was still being frantically wrestled into submission. Cameras 1, 2 and 3 had finally gotten their cables untangled. "Two minutes to air!" Now the studio lights came gloriously on, raising the interior candle power from about 15 to 175! A cheer went up from the crew, and my heart leaped! Hallelujah, we were a studio! It was actually going to happen— "One minute to air!" The next thing I knew, the film clip with our theme song was leading in, with Al Reimers providing the voice-over, inviting everyone to relax and join us for the next ninety minutes. There was Bob McKenzie frantically waving to me as I stood up in the audience, which was where we had decided that I would start from. I moved to my left, to get exactly where he wanted me, which was where Bill Bray, our director out in the mobile unit, was telling him. Now Bob was counting off the last seconds: "Ten—nine—eight—seven—six. . . ." And for the last five seconds, he did it silently, by throwing out five fingers, and then folding them down, one by one. Suddenly there were no fingers left. The red light of camera 3 blinked on. We were live! "Good morning, everyone! Welcome to an historic occasion. . . ."

CHAPTER 16

Stand Tall

From our side of the cameras, that first live telecast was a disaster! Everything that could conceivably go wrong, did. And yet we had to laugh: for instance, right in the middle of singer Brant Gillespie's first number, a volunteer cable puller, whose job it was to see that the cables to the cameras did not get tangled, was dutifully performing his assignment—and backing, bent over, slowly but inexorably into camera range. We all saw what was about to happen, and none of us could do anything about it. Unable to shout at him, Bob McKenzie was frantically waving at him, but to no avail. Soon his blue jeans were protruding prominently into the frame, camera right, and there they stayed. Someone *had* finally caught his eye, and he had frozen. Afterwards, I couldn't resist teasing Bob, "You got a little behind in your work this morning, eh?"

Unquestionably, the most trying assignment of all was that of Bill Bray, out in the mobile unit. As our director, he bore the final responsibility for the whole show. There he sat, in the eerie green-glow darkness, flanked by his switcher and his audio man in a space no bigger than the back of a bread van. The three of them were looking at a bank of TV monitoring screens, and there were wires going everywhere, and so many buttons and switches that it might have given pause to the flight engineer of a 747. Bill was oblivious to his surroundings, as he concentrated on the three screens which his cameras gave him, and from them tried to envision what was going on in the rest of the studio.

There had been no time to rehearse, no time to work with his crew or learn the studio; there weren't even lights until just before air time. Sometime during the night before, he had started to brief his cameramen, but as their eyes grew wider and wider, he decided they would just have to lean on Jesus like everyone else. He would be flying on instruments, unfamiliar instruments, and relying on the Holy Spirit more heavily than he ever had to during his professional career.

The moment the lead-in film clip began, it was like the starting gate of a horse race had sprung open. Everything began to happen at once, and it was all live; there was no going back to edit or re-shoot. What was done, was done, and then we had to move on. All Bill could do was to keep his mind focused a few seconds ahead, on what was *about* to happen, before it actually did. As it was, the present kept overlapping the future.

"All right, switch to camera 1—hold on David, number 1—that's it, now go in slowly for a close-up—slowly—stand by, number 2—switch to number 2—number 3, pan to the phones—number 1, cut to the audience—no, number 2, stay on David!—number 3, what are you doing? I asked for the phones—*you what?* You've got the cord wrapped around the camera? Well, get it unwrapped! Stand by, number 1, switch to number 1—that's good, number 1, a little more to the left—crop that woman who looks like a dog just bit her ankle—okay now, number 2, pull back and give me the whole interview set—and number 3, hurry up and get yourself untangled! Stand by, number 2, *what?* What do you mean, your zoom handle has fallen off?—Well, *get it fixed!* We've got only one camera left!—I guess you're it, number 1—number 1? Are you there, number 1?"

That was one nightmare I was glad not to know anything about; the ones I could see were bad enough! Like the time Norma-Jean was about to sing, and audio could not come up with her sound track accompaniment. There she stood, smiling bravely into the camera with the red light on, and no music to accompany her. Finally, they cut away from her to me, and I grinned and said something brilliant like, "Well, ha ha, growing pains," while Ann Hillsden dashed to the piano. Then I couldn't think of anything else to say, so I just called out, "Wing it, Norma-Jean!" And by the grace of God, she did.

That sort of thing has a tendency to make me uptight under the best of circumstances, and that morning I was really getting down, when, during Norma-Jean's song, Don Osborne came over to tell me, in amazement, "Don't worry, David, the Lord's covering everything! People are calling in by the dozens! They're getting saved all over Ontario! Listen to those phones!" And he was right; they were constantly ringing—every one of our phone counselors was busy. Praise God, "100

Huntley Street" was doing what it was supposed to!

When it was over, we all felt like we had just set the world indoor record for the mile. Happy and exhausted, we were too tired to sleep or think or do anything but talk about how happy we were, and how good God was. Our carpenter, Barry Mawer, had missed half the show; he had fallen asleep in the studio audience—his first sleep in three days. Bill Bray emerged from the mobile unit, looking like he had just come through the London blitz. He didn't hear the congratulations or feel the pats on the back, but when he came into the studio and looked around, he realized for the first time that it was a real studio—the first Christian studio in the country—and he cried.

We improved rapidly after that; in fact, Global was amazed at the high standard we were able to attain in just a few weeks. According to them, we were on a par with both of the two live shows from the States, though obviously we did not have the money to spend on a studio orchestra or elaborate production numbers. Yes, despite their assurances to the contrary, both "PTL Club" and the "700 Club" had come into Canada. I was shocked when it happened, but almost immediately I saw God's hand in what had happened to us. Now I understood why we had such a sense of urgency to get the program on the air, why the building lease and all the RCA equipment had fallen into place so miraculously. God knew that if there had been a three-month delay at the outset, and I had learned of their entry into Canadian television, I would have dropped all plans for "100 Huntley Street" and thrown all my weight behind their efforts, helping them in any way I could. Clearly, God intended Canada to have its own voice and witness.

For despite the surface similarity in format between our show and other daily, live-phone productions, there are significant differences. For one thing, on our program the on-air time is shared by myself, Don Osborne, Bob MacDougall, Geoffrey Shaw, Al Reimers, Clyde Williamson, Jim Poynter, and Gordon Williams—all of us born-again and Spirit-filled, ordained ministers. Considering our Pentecostal, Catholic, Anglican (Episcopal), United Church (Presbyterian, Methodist, and Congregational), Baptist, and Free Methodist backgrounds, it does seem to be a fulfillment of the prayer of Jesus: "When they see that they are one, they will believe, Father, that you sent me." For "100 Huntley Street" may well be the most visible expression of unity in the body of Christ in our nation today.

This working demonstration of unity is further borne out in our understanding of our call to build up the *whole* body of Christ. The truth is, we all feel that "100 Huntley Street' is a window to the body of Christ, and that God intends His children to work together in harmony, to the glory of His Son. The summer before last, three of our ministers attended the now-historic Charismatic Conference in Kansas City, where some 45,000 Christians of many denominations came together in true unity of spirit. In the mornings, the Presbyterians and Catholics and Mennonites and Messianic Jews and Baptists and Pentecostals and Episcopalians and Methodists and Lutherans met separately for their annual denominational meetings, but in the evenings everyone gathered in the Kansas City Chiefs' football stadium to praise and worship the Lord together. David du Plessis likened it to the twelve tribes of Israel who retained their tribal identities, but when they came together in worship, they were one nation—Israel.

Our men brought the spirit of Kansas City home with them, and it coincided with the way the Holy Spirit had been leading us all along. He was not calling us to forego our denominational identities or to merge our denominations in one; He was calling us to merge our hearts in one, and be one in Him. The "100 Huntley Street" family experiences that unity every morning at eight o'clock, when we gather in the chapel to pray together and share needs and turn the day over to the Lord. Sometimes Don will take the service, sometimes Clyde, sometimes Jim or Bob or Al, Geoffrey, Gordon or myself. But Jesus is at the center, and hopefully that's who people see, when we go on camera an hour-and-a-half later.

The area where we are the most unique is in our mission field. For in addition to providing daily Christian television, we are called to produce young people's programing of the very highest caliber—with no expectation of any remuneration. To date, we have produced 81 "Circle Square" programs, and 31 segments of our teen show, "Inside Track." We have channeled every dollar we could spare into this endeavor (and there are precious few spare dollars in Canada)—more than a million, all told. But the results speak for themselves. I have already shared the extraordinary reception accorded to "Circle Square" by Bermuda; it has been echoed practically everywhere we've introduced the program. And yet, in a sense, "Inside Track's" accomplishments are even more impressive, because the concept of the show itself is possibly the most difficult in the whole field of television: a Christian teenage travel and variety show that captures and holds the interest of worldly teenagers.

When Glen Rutledge took over as executive producer of "Circle Square," he was asked to broaden the concept of that show, to take in adolescents. He felt the need for this as deeply as I did. Every three days another Ontario teenager kills himself or herself in despair—and that rate is up 400 percent over what it was as we entered the sixties. Last year, in Toronto alone, 7,000 teenagers ran away from home. There had to be *something* that we, with our studio and our equipment and our committed staff, could do. And there was. But instead of an expansion of "Circle Square," the concept developed into an entirely new and fresh show. It features eight teenage boys and girls, who happen to believe there is a God, and His Son is named Jesus, and He is real. They don't talk much about that directly, for the intent of the show is pre-evangelism rather than evangelism, but they sing about Him, and He is at the center of how they react and interact. And their actions speak for themselves: these are young people for whom Jesus is their reason for living.

And live they do, usually at a very fast, quippy pace, for in addition to playing themselves, they are responsible for much of the production and idea-work under our capable producer/director, Malcolm Neal. And being closer to their potential audience than any of us in the over-thirty group, they know what will and won't work. One skit which they produced last year was a comedy set in the Old West, called "The Salvation of Ross Petal." Directed by our talented film-maker, Bruce Allen, it was obvious the cast was having an enormously good time, and their amusement communicated itself; the skit won first prize for the best short drama in the prestigious Long Island International Film Festival.

"Inside Track" and "Circle Square" complement one another beautifully. Because of the popularity of the latter, Bermuda will soon be broadcasting the former. And exactly the opposite has been the case in Hong Kong; there, it was "Inside Track" that paved the way for "Circle Square." This, then, is our mission field: the production of top quality Christian programing, without concern for financial return. Nor is it limited to young people's programing, for we will pioneer wherever the Lord leads.

Lately, He has been leading in some very interesting directions. We have just completed a series of thirteen half-hour shows for the deaf called

"Signs of the Times." Bob McKenzie has sparkplugged this project for us, and it has several very innovative features, not the least of which is that the show is done *in* sign language, for the primary benefit of the deaf, instead of having the words printed across the bottom of the screen, or someone making signs in the lower left-hand corner, for those deaf viewers who can't read. The show will feature deaf Christians sharing their testimonies and their problems, and just in case a viewer who can hear tunes in and wonders what is going on, there will be a voice-over in English, interpreting what is being said in sign language. Already requests are beginning to come from stations who want to carry "Signs of the Times" as a public service.

Another series along similar lines is "Au 100 Tuple," which is a French version of "100 Huntley Street," and which features French-Canadian singers, evangelists and others who have vibrant testimonies. At the moment, I am hosting the show with the help of an interpreter, but we anticipate the time when the Lord will send us just the right French-speaking host. And now in development is a derivative concept, with which we intend to reach new Canadians of a wide variety of ethnic backgrounds. For Canada is truly unique in this regard. Unlike the United States which became the universal melting pot, Canada has committed herself to helping her ethnic minorities to maintain their customs and heritage by promoting a mosaic pattern of cultural development. For instance, in Toronto alone, there are more Italians than there are in Florence, or Pisa, or Venice, and more are coming over to join them all the time. Thanks to Canada's encouragement of ethnic identities, they feel more or less at home.

But Canada is still an awfully big country, and many of its newcomers are bound to feel lonely or ill at ease. We will be providing programing in their native tongue that will set them at ease, *and* tell them about a friend with whom they need never feel lonely again. Nor will we limit our outreach to Italians. There are, in Toronto, seventeen other ethnic groups with populations exceeding thirty thousand! How do you say, "Come unto me, all ye that labour and are heavy laden, and I will give you rest," in Chinese?

Other than supporting "100 Huntley Street" and "Crossroads," this is where our money goes. You won't find it in lavish appointments; in fact, our visitors frequently ask us why our accommodations are so Spartan. The reason is because we all regard this work as a mission field—*our* mission field. Indeed, there is only one area where we do not economize, and that is in the tools of our trade: our electronic equipment is the finest in the business. A production does not have to be extravagant, but the end product must be as good as we can possibly make it. And that means maximum quality each step of the way.

Normally, I would not speak out in this fashion, but I feel it incumbent upon me, to let our viewers know where we stand. God has honored our obedience in this mission field and sufficient funds keep coming in. We spend them as fast as they arrive; in fact, as I've indicated, we usually manage to spend them a few days *before* they arrive. But that keeps us in a very needy place. If God is ever displeased with the basic attitude of our hearts, or our stewardship of what He has already given us, all He has to do is lift a tiny corner of the mantle of His grace, to bring us very quickly to our knees in repentance. If just a small percentage of our would-be supporters were to have second thoughts about sending in their checks next month—

It is also by the grace of God that we have never missed a payroll, although we have come mighty close a couple of times. Once, when Wally Riegert, the head of our administrative division, was comptroller as well, he had to make the agonizing decision to hold up the two-week paycheques of our more than a hundred employees. We didn't have even a hundreth of the payroll in our account. But as Wally prayed, the Lord seemed to be telling him to release the cheques anyway. It seemed like the height of fiscal irresponsibility, yet Wally knew that his first responsibility was to God. He released the cheques. That same morning, we received an anonymous donation for the exact amount of our payroll from someone in Ottawa, who could not possibly have known our desperate need at that point in time. It was the largest single donation, (other than the farms given for "Circle Square" ranches) we had ever received. We never did learn who he was, but if he is reading this book now, we all thank him from the bottom of our hearts, and know God will reward him many times for his own obedience to the leading of the Holy Spirit, if, indeed, He has not already done so. (Of course, if it was an angel—)

There was another time, however, when Wally actually did have to hold back the payroll cheques. It was in April of last year, one of those rare flukes in which three paydays fell due in the same month. Wally stood up in the little worship service we have every morning and said,

"Well, it seems the Lord is testing us, or has something else to say to us, because we don't have enough money to issue your paycheques."

"Hallelujah!" Marian Poynter shouted; others picked it up, and soon we were having the most incongruous praise session you could imagine! Tears came to my eyes, for I saw, as I had never seen before, just how much it was *their* ministry too, every one of them! The spirit of closeness continued throughout the week. Many people experienced little miracles of giving and caring for one another. Wally himself went to his mailbox the next day and found a receipt there for the final $300 payment due on his car. It was stamped "Paid in Full" by the car dealer, who was a member of his church and had heard what had happened. In fact, the story of our "no-pay celebration" had gone all over the country, and when the funds did come in, and cheques were issued four days later, several people came up to Wally and confessed they were actually a little disappointed.

Happily, unless we really stray from God's will, in another year or two we may not have to hold our breath as each payday approaches. After much prayer, we believe God has shown us unique and dramatic solutions to the problem of our comparatively narrow support base. (Canada has one-tenth the population of the United States, and one-twentieth her economic strength.) Thousands have joined what we call our Pioneer Partners Club for daily Christian television, contributing monthly and wearing with pride their "100 Huntley Street" pin. In addition, our supporters are getting together with others in their neighborhoods every couple of months or so for fellowship. There is nothing formal about these gatherings, and all who participate remain faithful to their local churches, but it is often a surprise to find that someone who lives right around the corner from you is a regular viewer of "100 Huntley Street," and you never realized they felt the same way about it.

We call these groups Local Community Councils, and twelve LCC's have sprung up in the past three months! If you are interested in starting or joining one, just drop Geoffrey Shaw a line, and he will put you in touch with someone, or put someone in touch with you. Who knows, it might be the lady three doors down, or across the street.

And so, on we go. Another offshoot of "Circle Square," is the Circle Square Ranch ministry which has blossomed under Reyn Rutledge's leadership. The idea for the Circle Square Ranches came as a means of providing person-to-person follow-up for the TV program. For that simple, spontaneous show was doing its job beyond all expectations. Thousands of children wrote to us, and many of them said they never knew Jesus was real before! *Now* what do we do? If they were adults, we could put them in touch with churches or prayer groups.

And then the idea came for a Christian ranch ministry where children would be offered outdoor fun in a Christian environment. Here, Reyn's experience with the King's Men in Australia, as they worked and sacrificed to start the Teen Ranch program down under, proved to be invaluable. We first introduced the concept of a Circle Square Ranch back in 1976, and as a private fleece we decided that if one suitable piece of property was donated as a result of that announcement, then we would proceed. In the next three months, *twelve* pieces of property were offered in different areas of the country. What a boost to our faith that was, as most of them were farms, worth a great deal. We accepted only those which we were actually prepared to develop, and this summer will see four ranches in operation, offering a lively mixture of horseback riding, hiking, a junior rodeo, in the quiet times a chance to get to know a real Jesus, and all the time, an opportunity to witness Him in the lives of the older staff members and assistants. And all for about half the cost of going to a conventional camp in a similar setting; we want to keep the camps as accessible as possible to the underprivileged.

Probably the most important development of all, in the less than two years that "100 Huntley Street" has been on the air, is our steadily increasing burden for our country, and our awareness of our need to call our countrymen to prayer. It began Dominion Day, 1977, when the Honorable Joseph R. Smallwood, the former premier who had led Newfoundland into Canada in 1949, was our guest of honor at a special outdoor celebration. He asked us to join him in a simple prayer: "God save Canada," and then added, "God, preserve the Confederation," and regardless of our private political affiliations or his, we sensed something prophetic in his words.

Last summer, in Newfoundland, I again heard him pray that prayer, and this time I knew God was saying to me: *Call Canada to prayer*. As soon as I got home, we launched our "Watch and Pray" drive, where individuals can write in and pledge a fifteen-minute segment of daily prayer at any time of the day and night. We will log their commitment, and should they ever feel that they cannot maintain it, all they need do is write and tell us, and we will withdraw their pledge. To date, we have some 256,000 minutes a day pledged, and the amount grows at an accelerating rate.

God gave us further encouragement along these lines last fall, when Billy Graham appeared on "100 Huntley Street" and said that, while Canada would never be a military superpower, or an economic superpower, she could become a spiritual superpower. "I believe Canada stands in a very unique position," he said on the air. "If Canada should have a spiritual awakening and a revival, the whole world would look to her. Canada could become the world leader in a spiritual dimension."

If you want to add your prayers to ours for this vital concern, do write and send us your prayer pledge. We'll send you a list of suggested prayer concerns on the back of your "Watch and Pray" card that will easily fill your fifteen minutes. We are entering into a time of spiritual darkness, more forbidding than the world has known in a thousand years. And if you think that is an exaggeration, take a good look at your newspaper. A new Dark Age is coming, and if we Christians are going to survive, we are going to have to stand up for Jesus, as we have never stood before! We *can* make a difference! There are still enough of us to influence public opinion. But we are going to have to stand tall.

And we are going to have to pray. God has promised that if we who call ourselves Christians and mean it, are willing to humble ourselves, and pray, and seek His face, and repent for those things which we keep doing that we know we shouldn't, He *will* hear our prayers, and *will* forgive our sins, and *will* ultimately heal our land. And God keeps His promises.

How rapidly the moral climate of this country has deteriorated—and at the same time what we can still do to curb it was brought dramatically home to us as recently as last month. Evangelist Ken Campbell was on our show, and while on camera he was overcome to the point of tears. The day before, at the request of the Crown Counsel, he had been sworn in as a witness at an obscenity trial in which a homosexual magazine was charged with publishing scurrilous and immoral material which encouraged pederasty, the seduction of young boys by men.

With my approval Ken called upon all concerned parents among our viewers to call the mayor of Toronto's office and lovingly express their concern, especially in light of the fact that during the trial, the mayor had appeared at a homosexual rally which had been called in support of this magazine. More than two thousand calls were taken by the mayor's office. I think everyone, including the media, were surprised at the concerted impact of public reaction.

They should not have been. Scarcely a year had passed since Immanuel Jacks, an eleven-year-old shoeshine boy was abducted by three homosexual bouncers from one of the Yonge Street body rub parlors. These three had perpetrated indescribably bestial acts on him and then murdered him, *filming* their atrocious deeds, to eventually show the film privately for large sums. When their crimes came to light, public outrage was so great that the body rub parlors and pornography shops were summarily closed. Aroused television viewers had joined their voices to that reaction, and now they were joining it again.

Every Christian who watched or phoned or prayed that day sensed there was a spiritual battle being fought for our city, of which the flesh and blood combatants played only a minor role. For the darkness I spoke of is coming sooner than many of us think. We cannot afford to put off our 100 per cent commitment another day! Ken sensed this, as he challenged our viewing audience to come out to Nathan Philips Square, on the following Sunday afternoon, and stand together in a rally of our own—not an anti-homosexual rally, as the militant homosexuals tried to make out, but a pro-children rally that affirmed the basic principles of the Christian family.

It was a bitter-cold day, that Sunday; the temperature was down around 0° F. and it was blowing snow. That morning my brother-in-law, Ralph, pastor of the Queensway Cathedral, invited me to address the congregation. I summed up the issue as I saw it, and then put them on the spot: "How many of you are willing to give up your Sunday afternoon naps and come downtown and stand out there in the cold and praise God and give witness to your support?" And then I did something I almost never do. "I'm going to ask you to raise your hands. I'm going to ask you to literally stand up and be counted." About half of them stood.

That afternoon, as we made ready to go out to the square, I had a moment of apprehension. But I prayed with a friend and was quickly reminded that God was in charge, and that thousands of prayers had gone up and were going up. And sure enough, when we got there, there were no pickets, no signs, no chanting, militant homosexuals. There were only a couple of thousand Christians, standing in the snow, singing hymns, expressing love, and occasionally clapping gloved hands together in muffled applause. But there they were, and they were standing tall.

Because I was one of the guest speakers at that rally, and because one of our national Saturday reruns at that time happened to be a program on which Anita Bryant had been our guest, "100 Huntley Street" was targeted for a retaliation, when we went out to Vancouver a few days later, for our annual stewardship rally. The first indication we had that something was amiss was a call that came in to our Vancouver office from the news room of one of the local radio stations, asking if it were true that Anita Bryant was going to be a surprise guest at our rally at the Orpheum Theatre that night. Frank Funk, our area director for British Columbia, assured them that it was *not* true, that we had no idea how the rumor had started, and that as far as we knew Anita was down in Florida, though we hadn't heard from her in months. Fifteen minutes later, the phone rang again. It was a different radio station with the same questions. Whoever was spreading the rumor was doing a thorough job.

I described the beginning of that evening, at the beginning of this book, how as we drove up to the beautiful Orpheum, we noticed a mob of pickets underneath the marquee; how they were carrying hate signs, "IF YOU LIKED HITLER, YOU'LL LOVE ANITA"; and how they made way for me and let me go in, when I told them, "God loves you, and I love you too."

Despite the hatred seething outside the theatre, a thousand or so men and women had braved a torrent of abuse and joined their hearts together in love and worship. We made it clear at the outset that night, that we did not hate homosexuals; on the contrary, we loved them in Jesus. But neither could we condone behaviour that God, in His Word, called an abomination. And, as it turned out, the media unanimously respected our position and our attitude. Even Laurier Lapierre, on whose talk show we were unable to appear because of a prior commitment in Victoria, rose to our defense.

The important thing is that that night in the Orpheum Theatre, after our initial explanation of what was going on outside and where we stood on the matter, we gave the militant homosexuals no further attention. We got the focus back on Jesus, where it belonged, and kept it there, despite a few attempts of hecklers to refocus that attention back on themselves. To God be the glory, His Son *was* glorified that night. Nor was there any further mention of the incident on our television show the next day or the day after. For we had learned something about the egos we were dealing with: they lusted for the limelight, and demanded that they be the centre. Deny them that by focusing on Jesus, and their hate loses its power.

But they were not to be easily denied. The next night a dozen of them were waiting for us outside the high school in Victoria where we were having a rally. This time, a reporter sympathetic to them interviewed them exclusively. She never came inside, never spoke to any of the members of our team or any of the dozen local clergy who turned out to support us. Nor did she interview any of the several hundred people who had also turned out. As a result, she came away with a very prejudiced picture, which she duly reported as an objective presentation.

Satan's frustration peaked on Saturday morning, just as the momentum of our television was also beginning to peak. The last four hours of our live, West Coast special, from noon to four o'clock, were the most crucial for us, and Satan knew it. And as he sometimes does, he fired his best shot, and then blew his cool. At about fifteen minutes before twelve, the station manager received an anonymous phone call, saying there was a bomb hidden in the building, and that it was set to go off at noon.

Four minutes later, as we were running a film clip, and everyone was catching their breath, the station manager told me what had happened, that the police had been summoned, and the station owners informed. He told me the owners had left the decision up to me, as to whether we would stay on the air, or evacuate the building. I prayed. And I recalled the time back in Hamilton, when I had rushed the gunman after he had wounded the hostage and the policeman. The thought in my mind then was that if now were the time my Father chose to call me home, then so be it. That same thought was in my mind now. I was about His business; if He wanted to call me home, I was ready to go.

But I could not make that decision for anyone else. The first thing I did was to go over to the studio audience. Thankful that it was a twelve-minute clip that was running, I calmly explained the situation to them, saying that I was staying, but that if anyone at all felt like leaving, they should certainly feel free to do so. Next, I told the CKVU cameramen that they could leave; I asked only that they leave their cameras on and locked in position. And finally, I told the phone counselors what was happening, and gave them the opportunity to leave also. Not a single person left!

As the minute hand approached the noon hour, there was no noticeable increase in tension; in fact, we got so involved with all the people coming to Christ, and the pledges coming in, that we forgot about it. And there was no mention over the air of what had transpired; that anonymous ego out there was going to be denied the gratification it so craved. There were two more anonymous phone calls that afternoon, two more bomb threats, and by the time the last one came, the station manager simply notified the caller that the police had been alerted to their call and hung up.

That stewardship week in Vancouver turned out to be the most successful we have ever had. And it was followed by similar successes in Edmonton and St. John, New Brunswick, and most recently in Sault Ste. Marie. It was clearly a spiritual victory, but it was only one battle; the war goes on, and as we continue on in His ministry, the forces of darkness are going to rise ever more strongly against us.

So we covet your prayers! We would ask you to pray for our protection, that God would hold us in the hollow of His hand and preserve us as He would the pupil of His eye. We would ask you also to pray for God to guide the media coverage we receive, that His Spirit of Truth would prevail, that He might select the reporters *He* wants, and then by His Spirit, direct what is written or said. Finally we would ask your prayers for the grace and strength it is going to take to carry on with the work He has called us to, no matter what the cost.

And rest assured, we will be praying the same for you!

For further information, please write to me at:

Crossroads Christian Communications, Inc.
100 Huntley Street
Toronto, Ontario   M4Y 2L1
Canada